A timely, insightful, short, well-organized, and highly readable book. Highly relevant to the themes of decolonization and democratization of power facing our world today.

Understanding the values, goals, and assumptions of others is at the heart of building a better world together. This insightful, research-based book will help you think, speak, and act in ways which lead to true collaboration for the benefit of us all.

Drawing from interviews with 90 leaders, this book contrasts the approaches, goals, and values of social entrepreneurs in the USA and Majority World. With numerous examples from various sectors and countries, Trice describes what's worked and what hasn't. In my twenty years of social investing, I have seen many of the issues described here. This book's findings and its practical recommendations are an invaluable resource for all budding as well as seasoned social entrepreneurs from the West wanting to build social enterprises in the Majority World.

Giving help should be fulfilling and receiving help should be a lasting delight. However, my cross-cultural social enterprise experiences attest to Dr. Trice's finding that friction, and in some cases hurt, are often unavoidable in these collaborations. The practices highlighted in this book will minimize our chances for hurt and increase opportunities for lasting fulfillment.

If we want lasting impact, we must courageously shift the locus of power to the people we seek to help so that they can more relevantly and sustainably control their own futures. Giving people today's meal may address an urgent need and make us feel better about ourselves, but that is not enough for them after we are gone. No one, rich or poor, wants to remain perpetually dependent on others' "help."

Dr. Trice provides a comprehensive, well-documented, insightful framework of how to re-think and tackle the tricky, entrenched challenge of partnering more wisely with the people we seek to help. She shows how to localize power where it really belongs, pointing the way to more sustainable impact and the lasting hope we all hunger for.

Randy Welsch, Co-Founder Jibu, Winner of the Financial Times Transformational Business Award

How do we bridge the gulf between us and them? Many American entrepreneurs may not be aware that such a gulf even exists. This is an insightful and practical book for any social entrepreneur seeking to bring about change in a community or culture that is not their own. It's packed with great real-life examples and useful solutions. Before charging forth blindly with good intentions, I'd strongly recommend reading this book.

Reuben Coulter, Social Entrepreneur, Investor, and Fellow of the World Economic Forum

In *Strong Together*, Trice has the courage and curiosity to hold up the cultural mirror on American and Majority World social enterprises to reveal what works, what doesn't, and why. It is no surprise that the author's cross-cultural immersion as a child— with a close up view of poverty—helped hone that curiosity as well as the keen observation and deep listening skills with which she interviews people around the world.

The book is a fascinating and transparent interrogation of her research findings, informed by Trice's multidisciplinary mindset and the indispensable voice of Majority World entrepreneurs themselves.

What Trice reveals in the process is a nuanced analysis of the complex and unacknowledged web of cultural frictions and power imbalances common to American efforts to "do good." Even more compelling are the insights into the creative and collaborative strengths—the cultural humility—of successful social entrepreneurs, which point us to meaningful practices that speak to our shared humanity.

Strong Together provides both the understanding and the practical steps that can engender hope for the dignity, empowerment, and flourishing of all—and that is what is needed to fuel sustainable development partnerships.

Everyone in development and its interlinking sectors, of any nationality, in any capacity from student, to investor, to policymaker will find this book foundational. The critical knowledge presented here has exciting transformational and peacebuilding potential!

Michèle Lewis O'Donnell, PsyD, Consulting Psychologist, Member Care Associates, Inc. and Representative to the United Nations for the World Federation for Mental Health

Having supported millions of women entrepreneurs to start, maintain, and grow their micro businesses in thousands of communities, we have learned the pitfalls of coming in with 'our' solution to 'their' problems. Dr. Trice's book challenges all to engage across cultures in a manner that respects local voices and recognizes the value of difference for forming fruitful, collaborative partnerships. This is a thought-provoking read for all who are trying their hand at social entrepreneurship around the world.

Atul Tandon, CEO, Opportunity International

In *Strong Together*, Andrea Nelson Trice speaks from and for the perspective of cross-cultural dialogue—as an anthropologist, a student of organizational behavior, and a person who has lived those lessons and commitments from her earliest days. Clear prose makes this book highly accessible and its probing discussion questions offer an opportunity for critical reflection—powerful as a means of shaping the reader's experience of the book as a growth journey.

Strong Together contributes to the understanding of organizational culture within international development, a perspective that is under-researched, and hence, under-recognized for its capacity to illuminate the challenges and potentials of our work. It gives practical appeal to the argument that any development enterprise must have patience and learning at its core.

The book gives voice to the critical lesson that social enterprise—and development more generally—carries very different expectations when it originates from within the communities it is meant to serve.

Nina Miller, Ph.D., Program Director, Master of Development Practice, Regis University

Dr. Trice's book speaks to the tensions that continue to exist between Global North and Global South approaches to partnerships. Empowerment, sustainability, and impact go together. For these to become desired outcomes, opportunity costs are called for. Intentional and relational partnerships have to be cultivated. Their value has to outweigh profit, quick turn-around, and ambition, which in most cases are the hallmarks of what would be applauded in entrepreneurship. May the reflection and action resulting from Dr. Trice's book contribute to building values and informing solutions to this tension.

Dr. Florence Muindi, President & CEO, Life in Abundance International, Kenya

As a young African leader in social and inclusive entrepreneurship, I was pleased to be interviewed for this book. Now, reading the inputs and views of others in this book, I find my own understanding of the issues broadened.

Wilfrid Marx Abidji, Co-Founder of SENS BENIN: (Social & Inclusive Business Ecosystem)

How often do we graduate young adults who possess great theoretical knowledge but lack cultural understanding as they seek to do good around the world? This research-based book uses the lenses of culture and of power to explain areas of common friction in international development work, amplifying Majority World voices to chart a more effective path forward. As someone who is deeply committed to intercultural learning, I highly recommend this book to anyone who leads globally-focused academic programs.

Michael A. Brzezinski, Ed.D., Vice President,
Global Partnerships and Programs, Purdue University

BUILDING PARTNERSHIPS ACROSS CULTURES IN AN AGE OF DISTRUST

Andrea Nelson Trice, PhD

GLOBAL
RESILIENCE
PUBLISHING

GLOBAL
RESILIENCE
PUBLISHING

An imprint of
Salt Desert Media Group Limited,
7 Mulgrave Chambers, 26 Mulgrave Rd,
Sutton SM2 6LE, England, UK.
Email: publisher@saltdesertmedia.com
Website: www.globalresiliencepub.com

ISBN 978-1-913738-62-4

Cover design by Suzanne Tulien
Typeset by Raghav Khattar

Printed and bound at Replika Press, Sonipat

To my children, Elliana and Nathan
May you each contribute to our world in beautiful ways.

Contents

Acknowledgments

Writing a book based upon interviews with 90 people is definitely not an individual undertaking. I am indebted to every person who generously shared their insights—and their hearts with me. Their names and their ideas appear throughout these pages.

Pamela Livingston Gifford offered fresh perspectives, important recommendations, and encouragement, particularly at both the beginning and the end of this project.

Ellie Hutchison Cervantes and Laura Belling conducted several interviews for this research project. Their work proved highly valuable to the final product.

Four people reviewed previous manuscript versions and provided invaluable feedback. Special thanks to Marigold Adu, Laud Basing, Leanna Giltmier, and Paul Nelson for offering insights that challenged my thinking and improved the book significantly.

Others provided answers to questions related to their specific field of expertise or connected me to people working in development around the world, including Heather Edwards, Rob and Anne Eyman, Roland Hoksbergen, Beverly Kellam, Tommy Lee, David Shockey, Kim Tan, and Galen Welsch. Thank you for sharing your knowledge and opening up your social networks to help move this project forward.

Finally, my deep appreciation to Kristin Poss and Elliana Trice who provided excellent editorial support and to Prabhu Guptara, my publisher, for his tremendous encouragement and commitment to this project.

Foreword

The exciting rise of social enterprises is one of the bright-spot trends of the twenty-first century. We all know of many social needs around the world crying out for attention. This has always been true. But traditionally the work of meeting unfilled human needs has been relegated to charities and increasingly overburdened governments. The brilliance of the social enterprise movement is its recognition that not every as-yet unsolved social problem must be written off as a "market failure" and left to the public sector to sort out.

Especially as technology advances, innovative approaches become possible, and more and more humanity-serving solutions can be generated by the private sector. Workable business models can be designed in many realms that make the solutions self-funding and sustainable. At the same time, it is increasingly possible to find sources of "patient capital"— investors who refrain from pressuring entrepreneurs to maximize returns in the short term, because they share their long-term commitment to alleviating social ills and advancing human progress.

So, there might be more truth than ever in a comment that Peter Drucker, that master of modern management, used to make: "Every single social and global issue of our day is a business opportunity in disguise." One academic recalled Drucker's saying this after hearing about his plans for a new research center to explore how socially responsible actions by companies could also be profitable. "Drucker, then 93, smiled and laughed at my misdirected enthusiasm," the man later wrote. "He told me I was asking the wrong question. It's not whether social responsibility can be profitable to business, he said, but rather how profitable business can make social responsibility."

The fact that so many young people today are determined to make the world better with their work is driving the rapid proliferation of social enterprises: top talent is highly mobile and gravitates to purpose-driven organizations. Also helping to fuel the trend is that the keys to managing these concerns are becoming less mysterious. These days, entering the words "managing a social enterprise" into a search engine returns many thousands of articles on the subject. As new ventures are constantly launched, every success (and failure) they experience adds lessons to the playbook on how to make the next social enterprise more viable.

An important part of that playbook, however, has been blank so far—a part especially needed by the social entrepreneurs who grew up in rich economies like America but are trying to have impact in poorer nations of the world. This is not a small percentage of the social entrepreneur population. While many focus on social problems in their own backyards, plenty of others want to make a difference far from home. And frankly, this is something we should all encourage, given the perennial disappointments of international aid. Social enterprises, in their effort to provide market-based solutions, can sidestep the bureaucratic, bloated, and sometimes corrupt machinery of governments and massive NGOs. They can be more experimental, agile, and customer-centric. Yet social enterprises also have their disadvantages, such as lacking the scale that would open doors to important in-country partnerships and lacking the established reputations that would help people trust their commitment over the long term.

The question is: What teachable skills and knowledge would help more of these social entrepreneurs—the ones who are not only focused on social ills but working in foreign lands—have the substantial positive impact they dream of?

In the pages that follow, Andrea Nelson Trice puts her finger on the deepest understanding required to manage social enterprises on foreign soil: founders should know that, among the members of the transnational groups they bring together, there are usually profound cultural differences that trip up collaboration. Going deep into the case histories of various social enterprises, she shows how the innovative solutions at the heart of them always sounded perfectly logical. Yet the road to implementing these clever ideas proved surprisingly rocky, as people raised in one culture struggled to work effectively with people from another.

Andrea makes a fascinating case that frictions arise because people from different cultures make very different assumptions about five aspects of their work together: whether decisions are more driven by the interests of "us" or "me"; how much it matters to make progress as fast as possible versus accomplish things eventually; the degree to which shared understanding of context means that communications can be subtle and still be understood; whether individuals should be expected to be relationally- or achievement-oriented; and how much value should be placed on innovation and the chance to try or have something new.

Considering this set of differences, rarely thought about by managers let alone tackled explicitly, I am reminded of another observation of Drucker's, made over half a century ago. "Because management deals with the integration of people in a common venture, it is deeply embedded in culture," he wrote in *The Effective Executive*. "*What* managers do in West Germany, in the United Kingdom, in the United States, in Japan, or in Brazil is exactly the same. *How* they do it may be quite different. One of the big challenges managers in a developing country face is to find and identify those parts of their own tradition, history, and culture that can be used as management building blocks." Drucker was born in Vienna, moved as a young adult to the United States, and once established as a management expert, spent a great deal of time advising executives in Japan. When he talked about the need to navigate through cultural differences, he was not speaking theoretically.

But there is a note that Andrea strikes that resonates even more strongly with Drucker's wisdom—especially because it features in the very title of her book. The way forward for rich-nation social entrepreneurs working in some region of the majority world, she stresses, is to capitalize on the *shared strengths* of the local teams they have formed. In the case of an artisanal venture in Ghana, for example, the strengths of the American founders were their business expertise and access to markets in multiple countries around the world. The strengths of the Ghanaians were the required artisanal skills and cultural knowledge of what organization structure would mesh with the values of Ghanaian workers. These made for a powerful combination, but only if managers knew how to integrate and build on them.

Drucker was absolutely convinced that managers must know how to combine and make the most of the varying strengths of their people. In fact, he defined it as the fundamental and unique purpose of the organization *to make strength productive.* That meant recognizing and using *all* available strengths—of people at all levels of the organization, and in outside partners. And it also meant not wasting resources to "fix" individuals' differences, viewing them as weaknesses or gaps to be closed. In any kind of organization—including the social enterprise—the most effective executives see and combine varying strengths as the building blocks of exceptional, joint performance.

Andrea Nelson Trice has her own great strengths to offer in her deep understanding of cultural factors, her skills as a storyteller, her networks and access to social entrepreneurs – and perhaps above all, her passion to help those enterprises succeed. If you are involved in social enterprise in any capacity, as a founder, an investor, a partner, or a researcher, you can now capitalize on these strengths in combination with your own. Look to *Strong Together* to get you closer to the impact you want to have—and the sustainable solutions your customers so greatly need.

— Richard Straub, Founder of the
Global Peter Drucker Forum
Vienna

Introduction

*"Probably more often than not, gringo is a term of
contempt used to refer to foreigners, especially Americans
and sometimes the British. However, it can also be used
with foreign friends as a term of affection."*

Gerald Erichsen

I spent my sixth-grade year in the Peruvian rainforest, and it
changed my life. Travelling with my family, I left behind my
Detroit suburb and observed raw poverty that stunned me.

We were in Peru with an NGO [non-governmental
organization] that served the local people in part by providing
medical services, teaching them to read, and breeding cattle
that could thrive in the rainforest. We lived simply in a small
house with a tin roof and windows that had only screens.
Our personal possessions consisted of what we had brought
on the plane.

I have very clear memories of watching the local people strip down to their underwear and bathe in a branch of the Amazon River that flowed by us. I remember laughter and light conversation more than anything else as I watched them shampoo their hair and try to rinse it clean in the muddy water. Even at eleven years of age, I experienced the disparity between what most Americans and these Peruvians had materially; the tension between the ease with which we lived in the United States and the physically challenging lives most of the local people experienced.

However, I don't recall being aware of personal tension between *los Peruanos* and *los gringos*. I heard the word "gringo" often. *Oye, gringo* was a fun way for us American kids to get each other's attention, and, to my recollection, Peruvians simply used "gringo" when referring to a white foreigner they did not know. I did not sense anything pejorative about the word—until someone explained to me that "gringo" was a shortened form of "Green, go home"—a plea to American military personnel in green who had entered Latin American countries in decades past. As a child, I remember trying to reconcile Americans' concern for and commitment to these Peruvians with this word that reflected, to at least some users, the frustration and even anger they felt toward the Americans in their midst.

This realization formed in me a question that has influenced my work ever since: *Many in the low- and middle-income countries of Asia, Africa, and Latin America, the Majority World,[1] feel frustration and even anger toward Americans. How can these emotions be reconciled with most Americans' genuine desire to help vulnerable people around the world?*

MY BACKGROUND

For the past three decades, I have considered aspects of this question from different angles. In college, I majored in Foreign Service and Spanish, studying cultures, political systems, and conflicts. After earning a master's degree in counseling, I worked as a university career counselor for five years. The university had a significant international student population, and I found myself developing seminars to help bridge the cultural gap for those who wanted to work in the United States. The question I explored during this period was: *How different are we?*

I hold a doctorate in Higher and Continuing Education with an emphasis in Organizational Behavior. For my dissertation, I was drawn to explore whether and how academic departments changed in response to enrolling large numbers of graduate international students. My driving question for this research: *What is the nature of power dynamics within organizations that include multiple cultures?*

Later, as a faculty member, I shifted from studying academic departments to studying international students themselves, exploring their experiences and perceptions of American college campuses. I also studied how status differentials affect faculty members and co-authored a book that argued respect for the least powerful members is essential if an organization is to operate optimally. My driving question during this period of my career: *How can power within organizations be equalized?*

PUTTING THIS RESEARCH IN CONTEXT

This book reflects my continued desire to understand and promote equity and to provide guidance on harnessing power for good. I am certainly not the first to explore power dynamics and to ask questions about the friction that often accompanies Western contributions to the Majority World, most often through aid. Key voices over the past three decades include two North Americans, a Zambian, and a Colombian.

Nina Munk, a Canadian-born journalist, sought to understand challenges raised by Western involvement in the Majority World by focusing specifically on economist Jeffrey Sachs' work in several countries. (Sachs authored *The End of Poverty: Economic Possibilities for Our Time* in 2005). In *The*

Idealist: Jeffrey Sachs and the Quest to End Poverty (2013), Munk identified Sachs' overconfidence and unwillingness to listen to aid recipients as contributors to the failed development projects he had led. He was, according to Munk, unwilling to tolerate dissent, marked by impatience, but attractive to many powerful Westerners who wanted a simple solution to a very complex problem.

William Easterly, an American economist, also studied patterns of failed aid. In *The White Man's Burden: Why the West's Efforts to Aid the Rest Have Done So Much Ill and So Little Good*, he concluded that two types of people work in the international development space:

> Planners determine what to supply; Searchers find out what is in demand … A Planner thinks he already knows the answers; he thinks of poverty as a technical engineering problem that his answers will solve. A Searcher admits he doesn't know the answers in advance; he believes that poverty is a complicated tangle of political, social, historical, institutional, and technological factors. A Searcher hopes to find answers to individual problems only by trial-and-error experimentation. A Planner believes outsiders know enough to impose solutions. A Searcher believes only insiders have enough knowledge to find solutions, and that most solutions must be homegrown.[2]

One of Easterly's key conclusions is this: "Only the self-reliant efforts of poor people and poor societies themselves can end poverty, borrowing the ideas and institutions from the West when it suits them to do so."[3]

Dambisa Moyo, a Zambian-born economist, explored international aid's role in African countries in *Dead Aid: Why Aid Is Not Working and How There Is a Better Way for Africa* (2009). She concluded that international aid had led to many countries' dependence on outside bodies, encouraged government corruption, and kept economies from achieving sustainable economic growth. Her recommendation was to end aid, forcing African nations to make themselves more attractive to private investment.

Finally, Colombian anthropologist Arturo Escobar in *Encountering Development: The Making and the Unmaking of the Third World* (1995) sought to understand both the roots and the role of development efforts in the "Third World" after World War II. His research led him to characterize development efforts as, "A growing will to transform drastically two-thirds of the world in the pursuit of the goal of material prosperity and economic progress."[4] In a 2011 revised edition of this book, he recommended instead "local agency," encouraging communities to tackle their own problems as well as allowing voices from these communities to shape the global development discussion.

A journalist, an anthropologist, and two economists have each identified misuses and abuses of Western power in the international development realm. As a result, most of these authors have called for people living in the Majority World to become self-reliant. The message, in many ways, is, "Green, go home," particularly as it relates to international aid. They have seen up close the results of misused power and they doubt Westerners' ability or willingness to reform.

Perhaps self-reliance is the simplest answer to misused Western power. But what is lost if we heed this advice to eliminate Western skills and assets from international development efforts? Rather than silence Western expertise in finance and business development, for example, are there ways to harness Western power so that it becomes a consistently valuable resource to people living in the Majority World?

I recognize using power wisely is a complex and challenging task. Sometimes it is impossible. But "leave us alone" seems to be a response rooted in hopelessness. It comes from concluding that the West's power will *only ever* be misused. With this research project, I hoped to identify reasons behind the friction that often occurs when Westerners work in the Majority World. I also hoped to identify examples, according to Majority World leaders, of Western power that has been harnessed for the common good.

My research focused on effective partnerships, emphasizing social enterprise within the broader development space. Stanford's Center for Social Innovation defines a social enterprise as "A novel solution to a social problem that is more effective, efficient, sustainable, or just than existing solutions and for which the value created accrues primarily to society as a whole rather than private individuals." Aid gives recipients few choices and little power—will I accept the aid, or will I reject it? Social enterprise turns recipients into consumers. I reasoned it would be easier to locate examples of productive partnerships in this context that begins with more evenly distributed power.

I limited the scope of my research to interviewing only Americans from the West, in addition to people from multiple Majority World countries, to learn about the struggles and frustrations that routinely occur in this space. I knew from the beginning that I would explore the implications of cultural differences with these struggles, so I chose to contrast only American culture with various Majority World cultures to make comparisons more manageable.

Throughout the book, I examine three primary questions:

1. *How and why do American and Majority World leaders differ in their approach and goals for building a social enterprise and for development more generally?*
2. *What are on-the-ground implications of these differences?*
3. *According to Majority World leaders, what are truly beneficial ways for Westerners to engage in the Majority World?*

BOOK OUTLINE

Contrasts are valuable because they can highlight unspoken assumptions as well as common strengths and weaknesses of distinct groups. This book is built around contrasting the approaches and perspectives of American and Majority World leaders working in the social enterprise space. It begins with an introduction to American international development and social enterprise work specifically (Chapter 1) and the ever-present risk of failure due in part to a lack of understanding of a community's priorities (Chapter 2). It then contrasts how American and Majority World entrepreneurs often differ in their approaches to building a social enterprise by considering two cases (Chapter 3). The book next explores culture's role in explaining these differences (Chapters 4 through 7).

Some Americans have studied a foreign culture, but few have stepped back and examined their own culture in any systematic way. These chapters incorporate research findings around five fundamental cross-cultural differences as well as observations about the American culture from Majority World leaders whom I interviewed. There are many other aspects of culture that I could have included. However, this section is not designed to cover cultural differences comprehensively but rather to help the reader become more aware of how cultural norms shape our approach to helping others.

Of central importance to this discussion is whether culture actually shapes one's definition of the problem to be solved through development work, the subject of Chapter 8. Chapter 9 looks more deeply at a common difference in our problem definitions—the relative importance of empowerment. Chapter 10 then considers differing assumptions that often drive our work.

Different cultures, problem statements, and approaches naturally cause tension. Seven common areas of friction identified through the interviews are described in Chapter 11, and Chapter 12 returns to the question of what problem is to be solved through social enterprise, and development work more generally, and the role of power in solving the problem. In doing so, the chapter considers the concept of flourishing and the extent to which the American culture is itself flourishing. Chapter 13 identifies several assets Majority World and American leaders often uniquely hold, according to Majority World leaders that I interviewed. Descriptions of five social enterprises that took a distinct approach to combining American and Majority World assets through partnership are presented in Chapters 14 through 18.

Chapter 19 explores three practical approaches leaders used to build these five enterprises that have been embraced by the intended benefactors. Chapter 20 considers facets of American culture that push against the notion of partnership and the book concludes by suggesting a path forward, based on the research, that can lead to greater flourishing for all involved (Chapter 21).

DETAILS ABOUT THE RESEARCH

I have studied culture's impact on organizational dynamics for over two decades. I did not approach this study with a blank slate. But while I approached this project with the assumption that cultural differences were at play in explaining friction that exists within the international development space, research from disciplines such as management, economics, sociology, and psychology informed this study as well.

I began the interviews using my personal networks.[5] Several of the first interviewees introduced me to others working in the field, who introduced me to others. The questions I asked changed and expanded as the research progressed, but they all centered around understanding differences in approaches to development, differences in assumptions, common barriers these leaders encountered, and common pathways to building a sustainable social enterprise.

The interviews were semi-structured throughout the study, allowing interviewees to share what they were most passionate about and allowing me to explore in the moment intriguing topics that they mentioned. The conversations averaged an hour in length.

Most people I communicated with face-to-face in the United States, some I interviewed using Skype and Zoom, and two I communicated with through voice recordings on WhatsApp. On four occasions, I also had the opportunity to talk with three to six interviewees at the same time, which led to some fascinating conversations.

A small number in rural areas of Africa, I am humbled to say, communicated with me by texting on their phone. I was amazed at their graciousness as they allowed me to ask question after question, sending probes to their responses, all the while communicating in what was for many a second or third language. In addition, two students studying international development conducted interviews with eleven American social entrepreneurs which added significantly to the project. In all, we conducted interviews and four focus groups with ninety people from Africa, Asia, the Caribbean, Latin America, and the United States.

I simultaneously collected and coded data, which allowed me to refine the questions I asked as the study unfolded. I also read through every interview transcript at three different points as I proceeded with the research and then as I began writing the final manuscript draft to be sure I was accurately capturing the whole of what I had heard. During the writing phase of this project, I checked back with several people I had interviewed to be certain I was capturing their ideas accurately. Once I had a complete draft, an American and two Ghanaians I had interviewed provided me with invaluable feedback.

Those I interviewed differed in many ways from each other. For example, their proximity to poverty, whether they lived in a rural or urban setting, their age, their faith perspective, their culture, and their gender all seemed to shape their views on the questions I posed. I have used their voices extensively throughout the book to allow these differences to come through.

A final word about the methods I used. Although in the United States secular and religious work are usually kept separate, I chose to bridge that divide in my desire to learn from as many perspectives as possible and to reflect the Majority World cultures that generally have far greater integration of the secular and the religious. This study, therefore, includes the voices of several pastors, many of whom serve as important advocates for the most vulnerable in their region.

AUDIENCE

This book is targeted toward people working in development, regardless of their nationality. It is for students of the field as well as practitioners. It is for evaluators building a conceptual framework from which to work and for investors looking for predictors of successful enterprises.

The research and ideas presented in this book will also be useful for those working with marginalized groups in the United States. Contrasting cultures across continents highlights stark differences that are not as easily seen when contrasting across American subgroups. But cultural and certainly power differences exist across American subgroups, and it is important to acknowledge that some Majority World challenges are present within the United States as well. For example, ten percent of American households experienced food insecurity in 2021[6] and 2.5 million children experience homelessness each year— one in every 30 children.[7] It is also estimated that 57 percent of Americans are unable to afford a $1,000 surprise expense.[8] As Americans grapple with dramatic inequities within their own borders, the findings from this study will provide valuable insights for building effective and equitable partnerships across American cultures as well.

Each of these audiences, students, entrepreneurs, investors, and evaluators, those working in a Majority World country and those working with marginalized groups in the United States, will benefit from a fresh look at the value of building together.

Section 1

Differences

When functioning in a culture that is not your own, the differences are palpable. Smells, sounds, mannerisms, language, food—the list of differences is almost endless. Our initial reaction is often to pull back and search for what is familiar, to isolate ourselves from the work of understanding and building relationships with people who view the world quite differently than we do. This approach seems much more efficient. And more comfortable.

But what if understanding our cultural differences led us to value them? What if we came to view cultural differences as varied threads that, when woven together, strengthen a fabric?

This first section explores cultural differences around such fundamental issues as how we view time and the value we place on group versus individual accomplishments. It builds a foundation for us to explore in Section Two the friction that often comes to the surface when Americans engage in development work in Majority World countries. Throughout this section, the driving questions are:

- How do American and Majority World leaders differ in their approach and goals for building a social enterprise specifically and for international development more broadly?
- How does culture help to explain these differences?
- What strengths might flow from our differences?

One

Is Innovation Enough?

"We live in a world in which we need to share responsibility.
It's easy to say, 'It's not my child, not my community, not
my world, not my problem.' Then there are those who see
the need and respond. I consider those people my heroes."

Fred Rogers

In 2021, Americans gave $485 billion to U.S. charities.[9] In 2014, U.S. private philanthropy contributed $44 billion specifically to Majority World countries.[10] Beyond monetary contributions, countless Americans choose a career based on a desire to help those in need. Anthropologist Edward Hall described Americans this way:

Americans can be extraordinarily generous to others. They contribute billions of dollars to charity each year … and are easily moved to respond to the misfortunes of others, both at home and abroad. This generosity is matched by no other country we know.[11]

EQUATION FOR SUCCESS

Americans are historically a generous people, but their preferred vehicle for helping others around the world has been shifting in recent years from charity and government aid to the possibilities social enterprise represents. Americans are coming to believe that the strengths of business can help communities develop in ways that nonprofits and governments simply cannot. Declining trust in the U.S. government is also likely spurring this growth as only 20 percent of Americans believe the government can be trusted to do what is right.[12]

It is estimated that 8 percent of the total U.S. population is involved in social start-ups.[13] People are disillusioned with the status quo, driven to make a difference with their lives, and for some, also attracted to the potential profits represented by the billions of people at the base of the pyramid.

These social enterprises or cause-driven businesses whose primary objective is to address a social problem, range from Kiva Microfunds, an online lending platform for low-income entrepreneurs around the world, to Envirofit, a producer of clean energy cookstoves. They are led by all kinds of people including recent retirees, those at mid-career looking for increased meaning in their work, young adults who want to positively influence the world through their work from the start, and serial entrepreneurs of all ages who have made millions of dollars and want to give back to society. Like their nonprofit counterparts, social enterprise leaders are typically driven by a desire to help the most vulnerable. They enter a community with great technical and business skills and a heartfelt commitment to make a positive difference in people's lives.

Several invitation-only organizations now assist the most promising of these social entrepreneurs, primarily by providing business coaching, mentoring, and opportunities to connect with potential investors. These organizations generally emphasize the development of a solid business idea, coaching from successful American businesspeople, and ample investment dollars as the key elements for a thriving social enterprise. Several leading business schools have created centers for social enterprise as well. They also tend to focus on the technical elements of the success equation by emphasizing, for example, strategy, impact investing, and scalability.

Technical skills, an innovative idea, drive. These are commonly deemed essential elements in the American equation for social enterprise success. But the human side is usually missing from the equation. This includes an understanding of how the host culture differs from the entrepreneur's culture and the confusion and frustration that can result from these differences. The human element also includes an understanding of power dynamics. Americans often enter a community believing they possess all that is needed to build a successful enterprise. They do not recognize, however, what they lack—an understanding of the local people's priorities, for example. Americans also do not recognize how the power they possess is often used to *drive* change rather than contribute to vulnerable individuals' growth and empowerment.

American Equation for Success

Innovation + Technical Skills + Drive ➡️ Social Enterprise Success

Compounding this problem, fast-moving Americans often quickly move away from a failed enterprise rather than learning from the missteps that led to its failure. Paul Nelson, retired CEO of The Crowell Trust, observed,

Almost all investors in social enterprise hope to be identified with successful initiatives that fundamentally change conditions for an underserved group of people.

Understandably, most are disappointed when their vision for systemic change fails to evolve. Terse assessment of the reasons the carefully planned enterprise failed rarely goes beyond disappointment with local leadership or lack of community ownership. Rather than looking for wide-ranging answers that might salvage this truly essential project, investors tend to just walk away. For their part, most social entrepreneurs move on to new ventures with similar hope for fundamental change but with limited insight into the false assumptions and blind spots that almost predetermined the previous initiative's disappointment.

It is at this point that calls to "leave us alone" may be heard from the community. But I do not believe this is the only viable response. Building an enterprise is challenging work, whether it is on one's home soil or foreign soil. Tapping Americans' innovative ideas and strategic thinking could be a tremendous boon to the work. To contribute more effectively, however, Americans must gain an understanding of underserved individuals' assets and goals and how culture shapes them. They must also wrestle with the power dynamics that are often at play when Americans enter a community.

The following chapter presents the case of an enterprise that had tremendous promise in terms of leaders' innovation, drive, and technical skills. In many ways, the case showcases the West's greatest strengths. But it is also an example of unchecked assumptions and missteps that too often plague social entrepreneurs and others involved in development work. And in the end, it is a case of failure.

PERSPECTIVES

One or two questions end most chapters. These are designed to provoke thought and help you apply the chapter material to your work.

The United States is economically prosperous. Americans who have benefitted from this prosperity have a responsibility to share their knowledge and skills with others.

Do you believe this statement is accurate? Are there ways in which cutting edge business and technical skills might be detrimental to the goal of helping vulnerable people?

What do you believe is the most powerful argument for Americans remaining engaged in development activities at home and around the world?

Two

Healthy Living

*"If you don't understand American's strengths,
then you don't understand why they struggle so much
to help other people's weaknesses."*

James Owolabi

Sometimes exceptional drive, the most advanced skills, and great innovation are not enough to achieve success in the development realm. Building an enterprise that brings about positive change, is sustainable, and is embraced by the people it is intended to help often demands more, as the following case illustrates.

Thomas Edwards co-led Healthy Living [pseudonyms], a social enterprise that provided clean, affordable water for urban customers through a subscription business. Ultimately, the vision was to provide a full line of healthy products, but initially, leaders focused on treating and bottling safe drinking water.

Before taking on this role, Edwards, a Westerner, had lived for a year in the slums of this East African city working with a locally-based NGO. He is married to a national and from his perspective, "I know more than many [nationals] who have been educated overseas and are starting social enterprises as well. They have not spent time like I have in the slums. They are from a very different class." Edwards' background brings important credibility to his reflections about this social enterprise.

Healthy Living was backed by two players in the clean water space and by a multinational corporate sponsor. Before the social enterprise launched, leaders brought in an American human design group to do market research and create a business model. The design team spent two weeks in the city conducting interviews with local leaders and twenty potential customers. A few months after Healthy Living launched in two locations, an MBA student from a prestigious American university spent three weeks studying the enterprise to develop financial models and determine how it could scale.

This social enterprise was backed by some of the best resources the West had to offer, but when we spoke, Edwards was beginning the process of "winding it up." The stores weren't making enough money and "there was not the interest there to keep funding this." What happened?

First, Edwards indicated that the enterprise's leaders had a grand vision—perhaps to their detriment. In his opinion, they focused too much on developing their complex model. Without meaning to create it, theirs was a culture that prioritized innovation over understanding the people they were trying to serve:

> We had a complicated model … We tried to do too much. We had a guy come for three weeks to do an internship. He was very smart, had built financial models for over five years in New York. What he said was right. His brief was good, but he missed the mark. His financial models didn't help us either. He did great work—interviewed

people while he was here. His report did help, but it's the issue of theory versus practice.

That's why you test. Why you take a cool model and assume there's more to learn, assume there are gaps in the model. Lots in hindsight that I wish we'd done. "You can't bring developed market solutions to a developing market." I thought that was a good line I heard somewhere.

A friend did something smart. They set up shop for a year and let it sit there. They learned from it. Tried bunches of things ... What we're actually finding is this ... I wish our consultants had brought in a culture of testing, had been willing to see things not succeed, and be okay with that.

The drive that characterizes many Americans also turned out to be a detriment to the enterprise according to Edwards, as leaders emphasized rapid growth over disciplined learning:

We went very quickly. In hindsight, too fast. We set up two stores very quickly and created something that was very hard to manage. We thought we were piloting and testing, but when you focus on the bottom line, there's such a rush. We should have slowed down, gotten our ducks in a row in terms of basic understanding of the market we were in. We should have spent more time on H.R., on training. We should have not cared about the bottom line for at least a year.

Our initial goal was to have a national co-manage the venture. She backed out, so I was brought in instead. A while back my partner said, "No way we'd be as far along if it had been me and her instead of me and you." But in hindsight, it wouldn't have been a bad thing.

Local people would have slowed us down, which would have been helpful. The rest of my team is [national]. I'm the only Westerner. Sales, marketing, and finance leads are [nationals]. Everyone above me was [non-national]. Maybe we should have brought in a [national] board, a steering committee. That would have slowed us down.

Third, Edwards reflected on the mismatch between the consultants' analytical skills and this foreign context:

Our outside consultants were involved from the beginning and put together a business model. The model started with a set of assumptions based on two weeks of research with key leaders and with potential users. It was a cool model but what they called "key findings" should have been called "assumptions" so they would be tested.

1. Clean water is always the driver.
    Reality is—not necessarily. If things are tight, clean water can go. There are other sources of water you can go to that are cheaper if you don't have enough money that month.
2. People trust strong brands.
    That's true, but if another brand comes along that's cheaper, they could well just jump to that brand.
3. Women are the champions of the household.
    They are, and they're more focused on health, but they don't always control the purse strings. If a husband says, "We don't have money this month," then we don't. And we won't be spending the money we do have on clean water.
4. People are willing to pay in advance.
    That's where the subscription plan came from. I hate that one. It's tough for people with little money. I don't need more water this Monday. I'm not finished yet with what I have. Or I ran out last Thursday and don't want to wait until you deliver it next week. The consulting group compared it to mobile phone

charging where subscriptions do work. But water ends up being different.

Locals were on the [human design group] research team, but it was mostly Westerners who ran it. I suspect locals made the connections for the interviews, but they did not provide input about the assumptions as part of their role.

If I had engaged [nationals] from the parent organization, it could have been helpful. We were too siloed, too detached from the national team. You sit in the same office but don't engage on local context.

You need a local person who understands the score. Not just on the ground, in the store working with the customers. You also need a local who is a tax consultant, who could help poke holes in the model for three weeks, who could step back and look at the issues, the concerns with the model. That could have been so helpful, bringing in local people.

CONCLUSION

Innovation, drive, technical skills. Healthy Living leaders utilized each of these components of the assumed success equation, but the enterprise demanded more. It demanded insight as to why financial models that had worked beautifully in New York City would not work in this location. It demanded an understanding of why focus groups, as Americans had designed them, would not yield the information leaders needed as they created their business model. It demanded insights about the people with whom they were trying to do business and just how much they differed from organizational leaders in terms of their values and priorities.

Americans do not enter a location with the intent to fail, but according to Majority World leaders I interviewed, this is what regularly happens. To build something that will bring about lasting, positive change, this complex but crucial human element of the success equation must be accounted for. Toward this end, the next five chapters explore differences in values, goals, and assumptions that often exist between Americans and individuals from Majority World countries and the implications of these differences for enterprise success.

PERSPECTIVES

What additional information would you like to have about this case?

Based on the information that you do have, does Healthy Living's failure surprise you? Why or why not?

In your opinion, what was Healthy Living's most significant misstep? Why?

Are you familiar with failed enterprises based in the United States that shared a similar story?

Three

Contrasts

"Put light against light—you have nothing.
Put dark against dark—you have nothing.
It's the contrast of light and dark that
each gives the other one meaning."

Bob Ross

Comparison is a powerful way to identify differences in the values, goals, and assumptions that drive our work. This chapter presents two social enterprises, one started by an American and one by two East Africans. The differences between these leaders and their enterprises are substantial, including the scale of their vision, their goals, and the ways they engage the people they hope to support. I describe the American enterprise first.

AN AMERICAN ENTERPRISE

Launched in 2010, Bright Lights [a pseudonym] produces solar lights that are manufactured in China for in-country partners around the world to distribute. The lights are high in quality but relatively low cost.

The enterprise was born from Mike Wall's [a pseudonym] desire to improve the lives of those who are dependent on kerosene and other fuels for light. In Wall's words,

> Imagine life without electricity. Picture yourself in a mud hut with a tin roof—soot so thick that you avoid touching the walls. Picture a lamp burning kerosene, its emissions of black carbon, unburned kerosene, and known carcinogens filling the room. Do you smell the burning kerosene and taste the soot as it is pulled into your lungs? No human should live like this.

Starting Bright Lights was appealing to Wall on a personal level.

> I love solving problems, inventing, product design. I was looking for the largest opportunity to contribute to a better world. Solar lights were a new concept back when I started Bright Lights. … I'm doing the right thing. We've sold 1.5 million. That's ten million lives that are impacted forever as a result of having these.

I asked about distribution.

> There is not a consistent way of meeting potential partners and deeming their trust. It's this patchwork of random interactions with me or someone who came to know Bright Lights through some press we received.

Keeping them is the hard part. There's a guy doing business in Kenya. He has an MBA from George Washington. We thought that would be the right bridge. It wasn't. In Haiti, we have a nonprofit partner. We hired entrepreneurs to do training with them. It hasn't grown up.

I sent staff into countries to try to be a liaison. I had a Ugandan who came and worked in our office here for nine months. He said, "Mike, I can't do anything else here. I want to live in Kampala." We paid for a house, his travel there, travel for his family. In six months, we got some traction, but it just wasn't working financially. We gave him severance pay and flew him and his family back to the States.

We've looked at multi-level marketing—Amway, Avon, affiliate sales. This is how things can scale and how you can get into new markets. Everyone who has tried this type of marketing has failed. There's very little that can be done. What works in one village will not work in another. What works in Tanzania I guarantee you will not work in Rwanda. You can map across a little more in the U.S. from Cleveland to another city, but things are just too different across cultures.

At this point, a significant part of Bright Light's sales are to nonprofits who give the lights away:

Solar lights—people will buy them in theory, but the reality is you have to get them motivated, get them familiar with the technology. Why rush to the paid platform? What's so bad about aid? Honestly, these markets don't exist so why not stimulate the market to begin with? You're not putting people out of business by introducing light because there aren't light producers there now and kerosene sellers don't make much off of their sales.

A MAJORITY WORLD ENTERPRISE

Bright Light's story differs substantially from the way many nationally led social enterprises are conceived and launched. Begun in 2010, Life Medical Services [a pseudonym] is delivering affordable health care in rural East Africa to those who have limited economic resources. Dr. George and his wife Lois [pseudonyms], both East Africans, have built a team of thirty staff members who provide health education and medical services. In Dr. George's words, they started Life Medical Services because of his past experiences:

> When I was in my teens, I developed chronic migraines. I spent one-and-a-half months at the hospital trying to access services. It took two more months to get the report, and it took two years to get a diagnosis [of potentially fatal cerebral malaria]. Also, my mother got married at thirteen years of age and she had eleven children. My father abandoned her, so she had to take care of us. That also speaks to my reason to support children.
>
> After medical school, I got involved in research in rural communities with the World Health Organization. Medical services were very poor. People had to wait in lines for long periods of time. They walked a long way to get services. There is one doctor for every 46,000 patients in rural areas. Life Medical is in a semi-urban area. We do outreaches in rural areas. When we see complicated cases, we invite them to our small city for services.

"What are your organization's values?" I asked.

> We treat every person. We believe that patients are our bosses. Without them, we would not have a hospital. We believe in medical transparency, being honest with the patients. We believe that by treating patients, we are

extending God's healing hand to them. We provide health care with dignity.

"How do you market Life Medical Services?"

We talk on radio talk shows. We do medical outreach in the villages. We do not charge when we are there. Our payment model is based on their ability to pay at the hospital.

"You have several partnerships now. Have you had them since Life Medical Services began?"

We started from scratch, using our own capital. Along the way, partnerships started coming in with various government hospitals and other organizations. We can keep our fees low because these partners pay above our normal prices for services. We had someone who was interested in having equity in our hospital, but it seemed to be more like he had a surface interest. He didn't have buy-in to our vision, so we said no.

"How do you measure success?"

We look at what changes we make in the communities— maternal deaths, schoolgirls dropping out, how many can stay in school.

"Do you feel a sense of urgency to expand your work?"

There is a sense of urgency to expand. We get patients from as far as forty kilometers away. When we hear someone was expecting and died on the way, that's heartbreaking.

THE CONTRASTS

While every social enterprise is unique, there are often common features that reflect the founder's culture. Bright Lights, an American-led social enterprise, articulates a broad vision of selling solar lights across the Majority World. Given this scale, interaction with customers is very limited. The founder designed a new technology that he believes will improve people's lives, especially by increasing productivity through being able to study and work after dark with these lights. As we will explore in the next few chapters, these characteristics are consistent with several aspects of the American culture.

Life Medical Services likewise reflects Dr. and Mrs. George's culture. Their vision is to provide medical services for a specific region of their country rather than providing services across the country or the continent. Interaction with their customers is extensive and long-term as they provide care and training in villages and in the hospital located in a nearby community. They focus on allowing people to live more securely in their current way of life rather than hoping to change their level of productivity or the role of work in their lives as Bright Lights does. Their innovation is "providing health care with dignity," something that was not available to Dr. George when he needed care as a child. Given their intimate knowledge of poverty and vulnerability, they place a strong emphasis on building hope and individual empowerment as they carry out Life's mission.

Culture is an extremely powerful force in shaping our behavior. A classic definition of culture is "that complex whole which includes knowledge, belief, art, law, morals, custom, and any other capabilities and habits acquired by man as a member of society."[14] Ken Myers insightfully expanded this definition. "Cultures may be said to exist for the sake of passing on from one generation to the next a vision of life well lived, a set of loyalties, a body of wisdom."[15]

Because we are usually unaware of its influence on us, Geert Hofstede, a leading scholar on culture, believes "Culture can be only used meaningfully by comparison."[16] Only after we recognize how differently others think and act from us can we begin to understand the way cultural assumptions permeate our lives.

The next four chapters explore common contrasts between American- and Majority World-led enterprises by looking at five important ways cultures differ and how these differences influence one's approach to building an enterprise.

- Whether a culture approaches life from a "we" or "I" framework
- How a culture views time
- The extent to which a culture is "high" or "low" context
- Whether a culture is more relationally- or achievement-oriented
- The extent to which a culture values innovation and the "new"

PERSPECTIVES

Introducing innovation from outside a culture is often the most effective way to bring about positive, lasting change in a community or society.

To what extent do you believe this statement is accurate? Why?

What do you see as the most significant difference between Bright Lights and Life Medical Services? What do you perceive to be the key assets Wall and the Georges bring to their enterprises?

Four

I or We?

"Most Kenyan businesses are family-owned, not individually-owned. There are wealthy families, not wealthy individuals."

Reagan Siamito

D o you think in terms of "I" or "we"? Do you approach your work primarily as an individual or as one member of a strong collective? The implications of your answer are tremendous as you build an enterprise.

INDIVIDUALISM

Americans generally value independent thinking and commonly assume we can accomplish a goal on our own, without needing to partner with others. Common American sayings and quotes reflect this individualism:

- God helps those who help themselves.
- If you want something done right, do it yourself.
- "Why fit in when you were born to stand out?"—Dr. Seuss
- "Remember always that you not only have the right to be an individual; you have an obligation to be one."—Eleanor Roosevelt

Individualism allows Americans to strike out on our own, take risks, and easily try new approaches to solving a problem. We don't have to go through the process of gaining group consensus when a great idea hits us. We aren't slowed down by constantly needing to negotiate relationships with extended family members. Instead, we have the freedom to pursue our dreams as best we see fit.

We try to pass this perspective on to our children as we raise them too. We want them to think for themselves and not be swayed by the crowd. We define courage in part as being willing to speak your mind. We reward individual initiative and are very comfortable recognizing individual achievements and contributions. Think about how many trophies, prizes, and certificates we give to our children for their individual performance.

Choices about where and with whom we live also reflect our individualistic tendencies. We speak of "launching" our children once they are out of high school. To us, adulthood means that our children should live independently, and extended family members may be quite removed from our daily lives. Retirement often finds us seeking a warm climate and forming new friendships instead of choosing to spend time reestablishing strong bonds with relatives.

WHAT'S IT LIKE TO THINK AS "WE"?

The American way of life stands in dramatic contrast to cultures where mutual dependence is highly valued, friendships are for life, and group harmony is crucial. For these societies, unity is a top priority. Children are socialized to think in terms of "we" rather than "I." They are taught that it is good to depend on others and to allow others to depend on them. They can expect friendships and family relationships to endure throughout their entire lives. Extended family and one's local ethnic group are key in-groups. At work, the collective product has the highest value, and receiving or pursuing individual recognition is not the norm. A person's identity is defined by his or her role in his or her primary group.

As Joachim Ewechu, co-founder and CEO of SHONA, an East African business development services company, explained to me,

> There's a different context—a communist stance to things that doesn't penetrate through to the economic side. People share. My tribe, there's a sense of community and belonging you have. That's why we have extended families versus nuclear families where it's everyone out for themselves.

James Owolabi, a Nigerian, expanded on these cultural differences for me:

> One of the mantras Americans say is, "I have a right to life, liberty, and the pursuit of happiness." All those things are personal, subjective principles. Other cultures would say the purpose of life is *our* communal tradition, *our* pursuit of life, liberty, and happiness. Before you get married, before you build a business, talk to all of us. What's good for us, the tribe, is what matters, not what is good for you alone.
>
> Say you are an American, you have a business in Africa, and you must send someone out of the country to work. In Africa, you can't just leave. You have responsibilities because you must care for your family.

That's what most Westerners don't understand. Family ties are stronger than business ties. In Africa, if a family member dies, you stop your work and you go to the funeral. Even if it is a relative you are not very close with, you go.

INDIVIDUALISM VS. COLLECTIVISM

The continuum below, based on research by Geert Hofstede, provides a picture of how people within various societies view themselves in relationship to others. Americans, according to Hofstede's research, represent the most individualistic culture in the world while people from many African, Latin American, and Asian cultures think and act far more collectively.[17]

Individualism/Collectivism Continuum

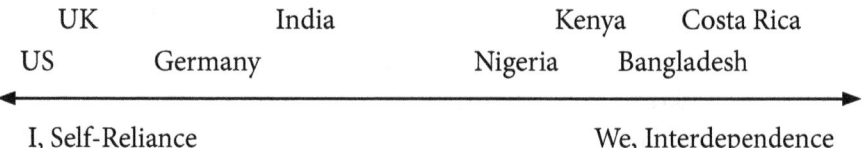

The table that follows highlights concrete differences identified through Hofstede's research on individualistic and collectivist cultures.[18] Is there a facet of building a social enterprise that is not affected by our individualist or collectivist orientation? How you train, manage, evaluate; what you assume about employees' priorities; how you think about job security; how company policy plays out; and how you communicate within a company—these are all deeply affected by culture. Even, according to Hofstede, our innovations, and the way we think about economies are shaped by this orientation:

Characteristics of Collectivist and Individualist Cultures

Collectivist Cultures	Individualist Cultures
• Collective interests should prevail	• Individual interests should prevail
• Value training and use of skills in jobs	• Value freedom and challenge in jobs
• Company has responsibility for employees	• Employees are responsible for themselves
• Group decisions preferred	• Individual decisions preferred
• More sensitive to shame due to in-group effects	• More sensitive to guilt due to individual effects
• Belonging is emphasized; membership is the ideal	• Individual initiative and achievement emphasized; leadership is the ideal
• Harmony should always be maintained, and confrontation avoided	• Honest people speak their mind
• Poor performance is cause for assignment to other tasks	• Poor performance is cause for dismissal
• Direct appraisal of performance threatens harmony	• Direct appraisal of performance improves efficiency
• Common in tropical and subtropical climates	• Common in moderate to cold climates

Technologies developed in Western individualistic settings more or less presuppose an individualistic mentality in entrepreneurs, managers, and workers, which is part of "modernity." ...[19]

Economics as a discipline was founded in Britain in the 18th century; among its founding fathers, Adam Smith (1723-90) stands out. Smith assumed that the pursuit of self-interest by individuals through an "invisible hand" would lead to the maximal wealth of nations. This is a highly individualistic idea from a country that still today ranks near the top on individualism. Economics has remained an individualistic science and most of its leading contributors have come from strongly individualistic nations, such as Britain and the United States. However, because of the individualistic assumptions on which they are based, economic theories as developed in the West are unlikely to apply in societies in which not individual interests but group interests prevail.[20]

COMPARISONS

Bright Lights, described in Chapter 3, reflects the individualistic American culture. Wall, the founder, designed a product after identifying a need that he could address. He read the research on kerosene usage, and energy usage more generally, as he built the company and developed a strategy for it. He formed a U.S. team, then established business relationships with distributors around the world who were charged with selling to individuals. When sales numbers were not what he needed them to be, Wall spoke honestly and openly with a Ugandan distributor and then released him from his role. As you compare his style with the Individualism/Collectivism table, it fits closely with Hofstede's descriptions of an individualistic approach.

Social entrepreneurs with whom I spoke from collectivist cultures tend to use strategies that reflect very different cultural norms. Mavis Thandizo Kanjadza, who started Kanjadza Acres in Malawi, is a great example. In Kanjadza's words,

> We take ladies eighteen to thirty-five years of age. We teach them how to grow things—we import a lot in Malawi—and give them one acre of land to farm. We don't give them money, just resources—seeds, etc. We make sure that whatever they grow, we sell for them. What they sell, that money goes back into the farm to allow them to start another crop.
>
> Some don't want to keep it going. They don't get money for their work and many don't want to keep coming. But two are left out of ten who start. They grow the melons, have success.
>
> They do this for a few seasons, and they are ready to grow on their own. Then hopefully they will be able to attract others to be part of this program or they will teach them. They will see they can earn $500 in three months, which is far better than $1 a day on tobacco.

Kanjadza's model is quite different from Wall's. Kanjadza Acres places a strong emphasis on training the women farmers and working in close, long-term proximity to them. A sense of group ownership is built as the leaders commit to selling whatever produce the farmers grow. Rather than providing direct appraisal, leaders allow the women to decide if they will remain with the program. They don't risk shaming farmers and their in-group by selecting those demonstrating the most talent for continuation. Rather they confer dignity and agency by allowing 80 percent to leave, recognizing that "hopefully [those who remain] will be able to attract others to be part of this program or they will teach them." Just as Bright Lights fits the individualistic descriptions in the Individualism/Collectivism table, this case from Malawi reflects the collectivist descriptors in the table, down to Kanjadza's extensive use of "we" rather than "I" during our interview.

People with collectivist and individualist orientations approach their work quite differently—and with different strengths. Collectivist cultures offer the wisdom of elders in decision-making and a life-long network of committed relationships. Leaders from these cultures also tend to have a deep understanding of customers and employees because they operate in close proximity to each other. Individualistic cultures, on the other hand, generally allow individuals to think and act "outside the box," to make quick decisions, and to speak openly and directly about perceived performance weaknesses. Both perspectives offer distinct value.

PERSPECTIVES

Heightened independence rather than interdependence is a universal goal.

Do you believe this statement is accurate? Are there drawbacks to the goal of heightened independence? What are the implications for an enterprise when a society's goal is, instead, increased interdependence?

How might a leadership team's orientation toward individualism or collectivism shape an organization in terms of its approach to training, decision-making, communication, and performance reviews?

Five

Who's Got Time?

To run is not necessarily to arrive.

Swahili proverb

Culture shapes our approach, our vision, and what we emphasize as we build a business. Culture also shapes the role that time plays for an organization.

TIME IS FINITE

Americans generally manage, save, and spend time precisely and carefully. Time is a precious commodity for us. We create GANTT charts, offer seminars, and publish entire books on how to manage time more effectively.

Think about how much we hate wasting time. We can choose an airline based on the percentage of on-time flights. We can choose an emergency room based on average wait time—now publicized on large billboards. We choose our path home from work based on travel times posted along the expressway. We walk fast, talk fast, and eat fast. We post clocks in highly visible places and are very aware when time is "slipping away."

American sayings reflect this view of time:

- Never put off until tomorrow what you can do today.
- The sooner the better.
- The early bird catches the worm.

To Americans, time is outside of us, something we think of in tangible terms, and something we usually want more of. Time is linear with a clear past, present, and future.

Linear Concept of Time

Past   Present   Future

From this perspective, according to linguist Richard Lewis:

[Time] flows fast, like a mountain river in the spring, and if you want to benefit from its passing, you have to move fast with it. Americans are people of action; they cannot bear to be idle. The past is over, but the present you can seize, parcel, and package and make it work for you in the immediate future.[21]

TIME IS INFINITE

People from Latin, African, and some Asian cultures, on the other hand, generally view time as less tangible than we do. As a result, sayings from these regions stand in stark contrast to the American view.

- Time is free. ~ Indian proverb
- Little by little one walks far. ~ Ecuadorian proverb
- Patience is the key which solves all problems. ~ Sudanese proverb

Rather than time flowing along a line of past, present, and future, people from these cultures experience time as a point at which relationships or events converge. According to Lewis again, "Time is event- or personality-related, a subjective commodity which can be manipulated, molded, stretched, or dispensed with, irrespective of what the clock says."[22]

From this perspective, time is an infinite commodity. Rather than a line, time is represented by a never-ending circle where time repeats. We don't serve time. Time is our servant and can always be adjusted to address people's needs. Therefore, present reality trumps appointments. The precise time we meet is irrelevant; the meeting itself is what matters.[23]

Circular Concept of Time

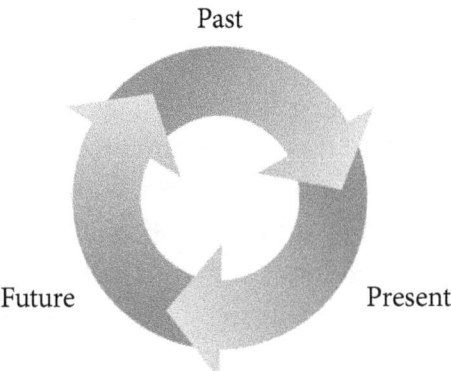

Past

Future   Present

CONTRAST ON THE GROUND

The continuum on the next page, compiled from multiple sources, illustrates how various cultures view time.[24, 25, 26]

Time Orientation Continuum

US	Germany		SE Asia	Middle East	Mexico	Africa India

◄───►

Time Is Linear, Finite   Time Is Flexible, Infinite

Because Americans view time as a precious, finite commodity, many Americans pour tremendous energy into building a social enterprise in a short period of time. This view was evident with the Healthy Living case presented in Chapter 2. An example with a far more positive outcome is Randy Welsch, a career entrepreneur, and his son Galen, who in 2012 had just returned from two years in Morocco with the Peace Corps. Together they decided to launch Jibu, a franchise-based clean water social enterprise in East Africa.

To build Jibu, Randy Welsch logged over 175,000 airline miles a year, worked at least 100 hours each week, and, in just six months, he pitched his social enterprise to 200 foundations and potential investors. Eight years into their work, Jibu had 2,100 retail points in seven countries.

Mavis Thandizo Kanjadza, who leads Kanjadza Acres in Malawi (described in the previous chapter), demonstrates a different pace. She mentors and works with women throughout several growing seasons. Although 80 percent drop out of the program, she is motivated by the fact that 20 percent are retained, and they will play a powerful role in recruiting more women to join. Kanjadza has built a program that, at least at its start, requires years of development for each farmer. Nevertheless, during our conversation, she never expressed the sense that the program lacked efficiency or that time could be better spent.

I'm not sure it's possible to over-emphasize the role one's view of time plays in building an enterprise and in development work generally. Certainly, individual temperaments play into rhythms as well, but cultural perspectives regarding time are powerful, as anyone who has worked in a culture with a different time orientation can attest.

HIGH AND LOW CONTEXT CULTURES

A third cultural dimension focuses on the amount of contextual information that is shared when communicating. High and low context cultural orientations, first conceptualized by Edward Hall, align with perspectives on time as well as with the individualism/collectivism dimension explored in the previous chapter. Americans move quickly and value efficiency. Many Americans also regularly interact with people who differ from them culturally. These characteristics naturally result in a clear, direct, low-context communication style. People from collectivist cultures, on the other hand, who have traditionally worked primarily with others from their in-group and who hold a more circular view of time tend to be high context in the way they communicate.

To quote Hall, "A high-context communication or message is one in which most of the information is either in the physical context or internalized in the person, while very little is in the coded, explicit, or transmitted part of the message."[27] Erin Meyer, a leading scholar on cultural differences, observes that in high-context cultures, good communication is much more sophisticated, implicit, layered, and nuanced. It's about picking up subtle messages. In low context cultures, on the other hand, communication tends to be much more explicit, simple, and to the point, which can come across as rude to those in high context cultures.

According to Meyer, geography and history help to explain how messages are communicated in a culture. Japan, the highest context culture in the world, is,

> an island society with a homogeneous population and thousands of years of shared history, during a significant

portion of which Japan was closed off from the rest of the world. Over these thousands of years, people became particularly skilled at picking up each other's messages.[28]

The United States, the lowest context culture in the world, is, on the other hand,

> a country with a mere few hundred years of shared history. [It] has been shaped by enormous inflows of immigrants from various countries around the world, all with different histories, different languages, and different backgrounds. Because they had little shared context, Americans learned quickly that if they wanted to pass a message, they had to make it as explicit and as clear as possible, with little room for ambiguity and misunderstanding.[29]

American speakers are trained to be very explicit as they communicate—they tell you what they are going to tell you, tell you their message, then tell you what they have told you. Written contracts are long and detailed compared with contracts in high-context cultures. It is important to clarify, however, that while U.S. culture is low context, Americans do also operate within high context settings such as families and other close-knit groups.

According to Meyer, countries vary significantly regarding context. "All the countries that speak Romance languages, including European countries like Italy, Spain, and France, and Latin American countries like Mexico, Brazil, and Argentina, fall to the middle right of the scale. …Many African and Asian countries fall even further right."[30] The graph below displays this variation.[31]

Context Continuum

US	Brazil Peru	India	Indonesia
	Mexico	Kenya	Japan

Low Context ←————————————————————→ High Context

This aspect of cultural contrast does not easily lend itself to a comparison of cases as I've done with the other cultural dimensions. What I can offer are two quotes from my interviews that may further bring this difference to life.

Daliso Chitundu, a Zambian social entrepreneur with a background in communication, shared, "We take our time. We do small talk in the beginning. Americans are straight forward."

James Owolabi, a Nigerian man now living in the United States, explained the difference to me this way:

> In American business, we say, "Don't tell me no." Sometimes in Africa, people must be able to tell you wait, so they can stop and think. It's very foreign. Most people won't tell you no. They will just wait till you exhaust all your resources, and then they use insurgent voices or nonverbal ways to tell you no. You will totally miss the cues. In non-Western cultures, one of the ways you say yes to people is when they come into a home, you offer them a drink. That's how we say yes, you're welcome.

Cues? These are something that Americans may not even know to look for.

The implications of these differences can run deep when it comes to a low-context, time-driven American working in a high-context, time-flexible culture. For example, Americans may interpret a relaxed view of time as an indicator of laziness or believe that power dynamics are at play when a national arrives late for a meeting or misses a deadline.

But these different cultural perspectives can also offer distinct strengths when combined on a team. People from a high-context culture bring an essential understanding of nonverbal communication to a team working in the culture. People from a low-context culture, on the other hand, articulate expectations and personal needs in ways that can lead to deeper understanding and appreciation for each member of a cross-cultural team.

Regarding orientation to time, Americans typically bring efficiency, drive, and a commitment to deadlines. On the other hand, those from cultures with a more fluid perspective of time often bring a greater commitment to building trust and long-term relationships among team members as well as with customers and clients.

PERSPECTIVES

It is appropriate for nationals to tell Americans they will deliver a product within stated timelines, even though they have no intention of doing so.

Think about your response to this statement, then discuss your thoughts with someone who has a different time orientation.

What effective and ineffective models have you observed of people operating in a culture that views time differently than they do?

If you are part of a team that includes people from high- and low-context cultures, who do you believe has the greater responsibility to bridge this significant cultural difference? Why?

Six

Achievement's Role

*"In America you work through the system.
In non-Western cultures, you don't get things done by working
with data. You work through people, through relationships."*

James Owolabi

A mericans are driven to succeed—and that's not all bad. How many more years might it have taken us to land on the moon if it hadn't been a race? Now there's a "race for the cure" for breast cancer and between 1975 and 2017, breast cancer mortality rates fell 40 percent.[32] Within the international development realm, how much has our drive to succeed motivated us to fight malaria? There were medicines to treat it and mosquito nets to deter it, so Americans joined the challenge, and the malaria mortality rate was cut in half between 2000 and 2015.[33]

Americans generally thrive on competition and define success by what we have achieved. We are willing to work long hours for years to make partner in a law firm. We uproot our family multiple times throughout a corporate career to secure the next promotion. We go to great lengths to assure our eight-year-old is the best she can be at soccer. We even have cupcake wars!

Isn't this drive and competitive spirit just human nature? Doesn't everyone define success in terms of what they've achieved? A website designed to help international students attending American universities describes these characteristics as distinctive of American culture:

> Americans are much more assertive than most international visitors. They use words as tools to express their opinions and to accomplish goals...[Y]ou will need to become more assertive and to speak out on your own behalf...In an interview, talk about your goals and accomplishments.[34]

COMPETING AND RELATING

How does culture shape our perspective about achievement and competition? The United States is what is termed a masculine society according to decades-long research by Geert Hofstede.[35] Comparatively speaking, people in masculine cultures tend to focus on success and achievement. There is an emphasis on mutual competition and performance and managers are expected to be decisive, assertive, and firm.

People in feminine societies, on the other hand, emphasize relationships and caring for others. They define success by their quality of life rather than by their achievements. Successful people are people who like what they do and work to live. There is an emphasis on solidarity and quality work-life, and managers are expected to deal with feelings and work toward consensus.

Hofstede's research identified several additional differences between masculine and feminine societies. The table that follows highlights these differences[36] and the continuum

Characteristics of Feminine and Masculine Societies

Feminine (Low Masculinity) Societies	High Masculinity Societies
• People and quality of life are important	• Money and possessions are important
• Emphasis on who you are	• Emphasis on what you do
• Beauty is found in the small and slow	• Beauty is found in the big and fast
• Boys and girls learn to be modest	• Boys and girls learn to be ambitious
• Work does not hold central role in a person's life space	• Work plays central role in a person's life space
• Homemade products are popular	• Manufactured products are popular
• Engine power of cars is irrelevant	• Engine power of cars is key
• Relationships and working conditions emphasized with employment	• Security, pay, and interesting work emphasized with employment
• Preference for working fewer hours	• Preference for higher pay

indicates just how much countries vary in terms of their priorities.[37] Because Majority World cultures fall all along the continuum, the implications of this cultural dimension for those working in development are muddier than others discussed in Chapters 4 and 5.

Masculine/Feminine Continuum

Costa Rica	East Africa		US	Philippines
	West Africa		India	Mexico

◄───►

Feminine,   Masculine,
Process-Oriented   Achievement-Oriented

It is also important to note that gender differences exist in every culture. According to Hofstede, "Surveys on the importance of work goals … show that almost universally women attach more importance to social goals such as relationships, helping others, and the physical environment, and men attach more importance to ego goals such as careers and money."[38]

American culture falls on the masculine side of the continuum and it is masculine cultural traits that have played a central role in building the U.S. economy. Americans do an outstanding job of setting ambitious goals that will have widespread impact—and quickly achieving them. These strengths also reveal themselves as Americans build social enterprises in the Majority World.

MASCULINE AND FEMININE APPROACHES TO SOCIAL ENTERPRISE

Healthy Living and Bright Lights, described in Chapters 2 and 3, are examples of a masculine approach because leaders focused on solving a material problem, hoped to operate on a very large scale, and emphasized getting the product into as many homes as possible. Life Medical Services is an example of a more feminine approach to social enterprise, because leaders focus on quality of life and operate on a much smaller scale with greater emphasis on relationships. The following case highlights an American-led feminine enterprise.

THE CAFÉ

Located in Southeast Asia, The Café [a pseudonym] trains survivors of sex trafficking in culinary arts. Site directors are married couples, as one of the women explained:

> We do this as it shows a really good example of a good, healthy relationship to our girls and, particularly in the field of sex trafficking, it's important for the girls to see what a good man looks like—and that they do exist. Aside from that, we are a fully female-led organization. All our national staff is female.

The baked goods the girls create are sold through The Café to the wealthy members of the city as well as to tourists. While engaged in the program, the girls also receive individual mentoring and life skills, literacy, and leadership training. Their mission is "to help restore dignity, hope, and a future to survivors of sex trafficking."

One of The Café's primary goals is for nationals to take on increasing leadership roles in the organization. Nationals currently conduct hospitality training for the girls and have lead positions in production and café management. According to an American woman who is part of the organization,

> We have an incredible team of nationals. They don't need us. What is one of the best things we have done? Empowering them, conveying that this is their business.

Every year we close for a few days to focus on building skills and building relationships amongst our staff on a weekend retreat. We make this a priority—going beyond day-to-day business. We invest a lot in leadership development. We send them to educational seminars, local events, etc.

With male leadership from a masculine culture, it is natural that Bright Light's focus would be on quantifiable goals, broad impact, and efficient use of resources. The Café's primarily female leadership, on the other hand, focuses on hand-made products and quality of life for each employee from the start. Leaders are highly relational and training that emphasizes each person's dignity, as well as mentoring, play a central role in achieving the organization's mission.

Bright Lights or The Café—neither approach is better. These enterprises are simply an important study in contrasts reflecting masculine and feminine orientations. And as with the cultural differences explored in the previous two chapters, each approach offers distinct strengths.

PERSPECTIVES

Establishing physical and emotional proximity with the people you are trying to help is essential for building a sustainable enterprise.

Develop a response to this statement, then talk with someone of the opposite gender to learn from their perspective.

Have you observed achievement-focused people who were also passionate about empowering others? Did they build strong relationships with those they hoped to empower or were they able to achieve their goals without doing so?

Seven

Starting Points

*"Twenty years from now you will be more disappointed
by the things you didn't do than by the ones you did do.
So, throw off the bowlines. Sail away from the safe harbor.
Catch the trade winds in your sails. Explore. Dream. Discover."*

Sarah Frances Brown

The final difference we'll explore in this first section of the book relates to the role people believe they can play in changing our world. How do our presumptions about our ability to control the environment differ across cultures? This chapter also explores how our diverse national histories shape our perspectives.

LOCUS OF CONTROL

Most Americans operate assuming an internal locus of control. *I* determine my future, not fate. Life is what *I* make of it. From this perspective, almost everything can be changed, and few things must simply be accepted. Given this mindset, Americans tend to approach challenges with optimism. Research has found that American entrepreneurs are especially optimistic[39] and alert to opportunities.[40, 41] Common American sayings reflect this optimism.

- Go for it!
- Grab the bull by the horns!
- What have I got to lose?

People from many cultures in the Majority World, on the other hand, assume an external locus of control. They believe that fate or a higher power plays a major role in determining the future. From this perspective, individuals are limited in their ability to shape their own destiny or external events. Instead, many aspects of life must simply be accepted. The sayings below reflect the perspective that life largely happens to you.

- We can't change the direction of the wind, but we can adjust the sails. ~ Indian proverb[42]
- He who is destined for power does not have to fight for it. ~ Ugandan proverb[43]
- A person born to be a flowerpot will not go beyond the porch. ~ Mexican proverb[44]

The continuum below was adapted from a book by Craig Storti who heads a cross-cultural training firm. He constructed this using input from nationals as well as the results of various intercultural surveys and studies.[45]

Locus of Control Continuum

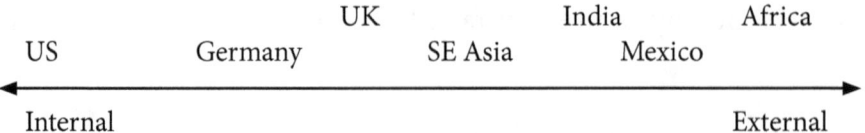

Americans and many from the Majority World approach initiatives with different cultural assumptions about what they do and do not control. The implications can be significant as they define their work.

AMERICAN STARTING POINTS

With an assumed internal locus of control, Americans tend to be optimistic about our ability to overcome challenges. This perspective is also influenced by our past. We are a country of pioneers and explorers. Our history began with the difficult, but ultimately successful, establishment of a democracy in the New World. We later headed west, successfully expanding to the next ocean (recognizing that this expansion came at a supremely high cost to Indigenous Americans). According to Nathan Myhrvold, former Chief Technology Officer at Microsoft, "American culture worships explorers—look at the fame of Lewis and Clark, for example."[46] More recently, space caught our collective imagination, including the race to the moon, and we enthusiastically and successfully pursued space travel.

The resources Americans have at hand no doubt contribute to our optimism as well. The United States has an advanced infrastructure that makes addressing global challenges easier. This is not the case for most living in the Majority World. Farrah, a Pakistani woman studying in the United States, described the American context to me this way:

> You have many more resources and opportunities here. If you want to help people in Kenya, you would find organizations that would fund you and give you a ticket to go there.
>
> Airline ticket prices in the U.S. are much cheaper than in Pakistan. There, applying for a visa is expensive and much more complicated, and you cannot do it online. I had to go to a different city five hours away from where I

was living. It took seven hours, the whole day, just to go for the interview for my visa. And then all the documentation and fees involved are on top of that.

Besides that, you know the U.S. government will be protecting you no matter where you are. You will not just be alone. That's not the case for most countries.

Some of the resources that Farrah described are not equally distributed within the U.S., but the fact is that many Americans who are involved with a Majority World social enterprise come from a privileged background. An article by Social Enterprise Alliance's CEO Kevin Lynch spoke powerfully to the social capital many bring to their work and to their outlook.

As Lynch described himself to the reader, he noted,

What you'd likely, but probably not even consciously notice, is the winner of an ostensible jackpot of demographic advantage: A straight, white, educated, suburban, professional, middle-class, currently-healthy, currently-abled, extremely well-fed male. I am the epitome and beneficiary of an extraordinary level of privilege that I did nothing to earn or deserve. Privilege that I have been slow to understand but quick to harness.[47]

Like Lynch, most Americans involved in development work have college degrees, often have travelled extensively or lived overseas, have minimal debt which allows them to work for relatively low pay, and do not have extended family members who are dependent upon them for financial support. In fact, several Americans I interviewed believe a substantial number of social entrepreneurs have accumulated so many personal resources that guilt is a major driver in their decision to engage in this work.

An internal locus of control, a national history of successfully overcoming significant challenges, and extensive resources at both the individual and societal level can all contribute to a strong sense of optimism in one's ability to address the needs of vulnerable people around the world.

Many Americans take this optimism a step further by framing their work as a battle they can fight and win. Key words commonly used in the development space reflect confrontation. "Impact," widely used to describe the contribution of an organization to a people or society, is synonymous with "clash" and "smash." "Strategy" has its origins in the Greek military words *stratos* "army" and *agein* "to lead," a scenario where victory is achieved by force.[48]

This battle mindset is reflected in the words Americans have historically used to talk about poverty within our own country. President Lyndon B. Johnson, in his State of the Union Address in 1964, introduced America's War on Poverty this way:

> This administration today, here and now, declares unconditional war on poverty in America ... It will not be a short or easy struggle, no single weapon or strategy will suffice, but we shall not rest until that war is won.... Our chief weapons in a more pinpointed attack will be better schools, and better health, and better homes, and better training, and better job opportunities.[49]

There could be many implications for those who embrace this notion of fighting a global battle against poverty. Strategic plans quickly become national or multinational in scope rather than regional or local. Goods are introduced into a society with an "aggressive" marketing plan. The work carries a constant sense of urgency, which Americans feel even more strongly because of their cultural emphasis on time's finiteness. From this frame of reference, the war on poverty can quickly become focused on a rapid, decisive victory rather than on the individuals whose lives are deeply affected by a myriad of challenges.

MAJORITY WORLD STARTING POINTS

The Majority World leaders I interviewed did not frame their work as a battle. Their understanding of the complex challenges facing their country or region led to a more restrained view of the future. It also led to a focus that generally extended beyond the problem of material poverty. Add to this perspective a national history that often includes domination by an outside power and the result was typically a very different characterization of the present "battle" and the wisest path forward.

Many Americans I interviewed expressed significant optimism as they entered a foreign environment and worked to create a solution to a complex problem. They had a strategy and skills that they believed would help them succeed. The nationals I interviewed, on the other hand, were more apt to express patience and the assumption that they must work alongside numerous others as they invested their lives in their people's future.

A scenario in which roles are reversed illustrates these different starting points. Envision someone from the Majority World moving to the United States to tackle the poverty that plagues many members of our society. The leader being optimistic enough to believe that he or she could not only impact a community but perhaps an entire region and do so in a relatively short period of time would surprise most Americans, to say the least.

In fact, a Nigerian man I interviewed did come to the United States to help address a challenge we face. His work reflects the patient, community-based approach I most often heard described by Majority World leaders. Since 2015, he has lived on the south side of Chicago, helping youth in his community find dignity and hope. His approach is highly relational, very local in scope, and he expects to live and work there for years to come. He is optimistic about the impact of his work, but his optimism is tempered by his understanding of the complex problems facing these young people. He is also confident about the value of his work but sees it as only one contribution among many made by a network of people living in this community.

Like the cultural differences described in the previous three chapters, variation in leaders' mindsets could represent distinct assets for a multinational team. Leaders who bring tremendous optimism and an internal locus of control may energetically move an enterprise forward. Those with greater on-the-ground insight may balance this optimism with essential cautions and lessons learned from others' failed attempts at similar change.

These different mindsets shape not only how American and Majority World leaders work, but also how they define the problem that needs to be solved. The next chapter explores this foundational issue of problem definition.

PERSPECTIVES

What additional implications of a battle mindset might there be for Americans working in either the United States or the Majority World? For those they are trying to help?

What might be a more useful metaphor to describe the work of addressing poverty's challenges around the world?

American-led social enterprises often fail because people do not understand what leaders are trying to accomplish.

Under what circumstances might this be a true statement? Under what circumstances might this be a false statement?

Section 2

The Problem to Be Solved

Many Americans' values differ in important ways from the values held by people living in the Majority World. Section Two considers the relationship between our values and the problem we identify as needing to be solved through our work. It also describes friction and power struggles that ensue when people operate from different problem definitions. The section then challenges the reader to consider these differences within the broader concept of societal and individual flourishing. The driving questions throughout Chapters 8 through 12 are:

- How and why do American and Majority World leaders differ in their definition of the problem that must be solved?
- What additional factors influence what American and Majority World social entrepreneurs build and how they build it?

Eight

Defining

*"If I had an hour to solve a problem,
I'd spend 55 minutes thinking about the problem
and five minutes thinking about solutions."*

Albert Einstein

Amerian culture differs from most Majority World cultures in significant ways. To ignore or dismiss these differences is to miss gaining crucial insight as to why tension often exists between Americans and the people we are trying to help.

DEFINING THE PROBLEM

Chapters 4 through 7 highlighted research indicating that Americans are generally individualistic and optimistic about our ability to overcome challenges, we view time as a scarce commodity, and men, in particular, tend to value accomplishing goals more than building long-term relationships. Many from the Majority World operate instead from a collectivist perspective, see time as something they control, and place a high value on long-term relationships built gradually upon trust.

These significant cultural differences can help to explain the different approaches to social entrepreneurship, and development work more generally, that I heard as I conducted the interviews for this study. But American and Majority World leaders' varying approaches are far more than stylistic preference. In many cases, they ultimately reflect different definitions of the problem to be solved through their work. The Americans I interviewed most often focused on solving a discrete material problem while the Majority World entrepreneurs generally focused on empowering individuals and communities. The following pages examine this difference using data from my interviews as well as multiple external sources.

Contrasting Social Enterprise Goals

American-Led Social Enterprises	Majority World-Led Social Enterprises
• Success often defined by addressing material needs; focused goals	• Success often defined by addressing human needs such as hope; holistic goals
• Focus on scaling; widespread impact	• Focus on community development; local impact
• Flourishing defined in economic terms	• Flourishing largely defined using human development terms (*e.g.*, empowerment, dignity)

AMERICANS' FOCUS

Most of the Americans I interviewed, particularly the men, came from a business or engineering background. They tended to define the problem to be solved in concrete terms—a lack of health services, unsafe drinking water, inadequate food sources, or unemployment. Some of these entrepreneurs had technical skills and access to an infrastructure that would allow them to develop and test new technology. Others had well-developed business skills they wanted to employ. All had a desire to help those who were less fortunate.

They generally focused at an aggregate level rather than trying to provide holistic support or training to individuals. Their goal was to introduce an innovation that would improve lives or to build a business that could generate income for employees and small business owners and thereby build the economy overall. They hoped to provide a valuable product to as many people as possible, and generally, it was not a priority to build personal relationships with their customers. The exceptions to this American approach were generally women.

I interviewed American female engineers who were developing medical screening devices and women who were building businesses that did not include holistic employee development. However, I also interviewed American women who engaged deeply with their customers and employees and prioritized building skills, hope, and self-respect in addition to working toward improved material conditions. The Café, highlighted in Chapter 6, is an example of this focus.

Given differences *among* American entrepreneurs, this discussion of different problem definitions must be approached carefully. Definitions did not strictly fall into one of two camps—American and Majority World. Nevertheless, *most* of the American entrepreneurs I interviewed focused on solving a discrete, material problem, which is characteristic of the broader social enterprise culture in the United States. Let me offer a few examples that reflect this common American conception of the problem.

AMERICAN MEDIA AND RESEARCH

David Bornstein is the author of the widely read *How to Change the World: Social Entrepreneurs and the Power of New Ideas* and the co-author of *Social Entrepreneurship: What Everyone Needs to Know*. He was also the co-creator of a weekly column in the *New York Times* called "Fixes" that looked at solutions to social problems and why they worked.[50] Problems, ranging from cholera to drought to the wealth gap, along with helpful approaches to solving them, were highlighted in essays. The title of the column itself reflected this focus on concrete, discrete issues.

The common equation for a successful social enterprise that many Americans use—an innovative idea, drive, and technical skills—fits this conceptualization of the problem as well. Human longings that go far beyond a desire for more material resources play no prominent role in the work of many business schools and accelerators designed to prepare and successfully launch social entrepreneurs for work around the world. Terms commonly used in the social enterprise space, "emerging markets," "developing markets," and "the poor," also reflect many Americans' focus on external, economically-defined challenges.

Americans' focus on material problems is also reflected in our approach to empirical research. Economists Lybbert and Wydick observed, "Until very recently, development economics has chosen an approach to poverty that has almost exclusively focused on the relief of external constraints, where these constraints might include credit, education, health, infrastructure and so forth."[51]

The following excerpts from behavioral economics which "consist[s] of systematic deviations from the standard economic model in terms of preferences, beliefs, and decision-making"[52] highlight these values as well. (Standard economic models, you may recall from Chapter 4, are largely Western in origin and therefore reflect Western cultural values and assumptions.)

In addressing the hesitancy of Majority World farmers to buy fertilizer that would increase their yield, scholars wrote: "Our model suggests small, time-limited discounts can potentially help present-biased farmers overcome procrastination problems, while minimally distorting the investment decisions of farmers who do not suffer from such problems."[53]

As part of a review of behavioral economics literature that sought to explain individuals' economic choices through psychological insights, the authors wrote, "Fully naïve individuals will not take advantage of commitment devices to overcome their self-control problems, while partially naïve individuals will mispredict whether a given commitment device is likely to work for them."[54]

These articles shed light on sense-making when trying to explain behaviors that are illogical if viewed through a Western lens focused on discrete, material problems. If the goal is an increase in material resources, then refusing fertilizer that would increase yield is irrational. But what is the fallout when we don't consider broader needs as a result of mislabeled behaviors?

AMERICAN EVALUATION

In addition to empirical research, the focus on material poverty and external constraints has been evident in Americans' common approach to measuring impact. For example, the Progress Out of Poverty Index, which was developed by the Washington, D.C.-based Grameen Foundation was "a poverty measurement tool for organizations and businesses with a mission to serve the poor."[55] The Foundation developed indices for the countries where 90 percent of the world's poorest people live. To measure whether people were climbing out of poverty, a country index might include the type of cooking fuel used and home construction materials as well as whether the individual owned a television,

DVD player, radio, car, or motorbike, depending on the country. With this instrument, progress was largely defined in terms of goods accumulation rather than also considering the agency and hope people possessed to improve their circumstances. (This instrument has since been rebranded the Poverty Probability Index and is now housed by Innovations for Poverty Action.)

Instruments point to assumptions regarding the problem to be solved. Resolution of a problem primarily defined by a lack of material resources would logically be measured by level of consumption—whether it is the consumption of clean water, electricity, televisions, or motorbikes.

THE AMERICAN DREAM

Fixes, external constraints, increased consumption. Why do many American social entrepreneurs focus on material problems rather than on human flourishing more broadly? Part of the answer may be purely practical. Material problems are simpler and faster to solve and the skill sets of many social entrepreneurs in particular are in management or engineering, rather than, for example, human resources. Part of the answer may also lie in our own definition of success.

Fox News conducted a survey asking people what they believe defines the American Dream today.[56] The top two responses were retiring comfortably and having a successful career. Some may wish the current definition of the American Dream was broader or different, but for now economic and career achievement seem to serve as its foundation.

The American Dream reflects cultural values—achievement, independence, opportunity, and material wealth to name a few. The Dream is part of our DNA, and it has doubtless influenced our rapid economic development. It is only natural that it would also shape the dream we have for others.

A DIFFERENT DREAM

Tension exists, however, because the Majority World leaders I interviewed most often focused on a need to enhance human as well as material resources. As part of their mission, these leaders frequently offer training based on what their employees or customers indicate they need and want. They also invest in ways to bolster individuals' agency. Certainly, they hope to increase people's material resources, but for many leaders, this is not their highest goal.

An example is Linda Mukangoga who co-leads Haute Baso, a fashion enterprise. A Rwandan, she spent most of her youth in Washington D.C. because of the civil war at home. Mukangoga started the company in 2014, emphasizing the holistic development of her employees. The organization's website states, "Haute Baso recognized the potential of young women by offering them training and employment—an investment which results in skill development at a fair wage and within a safe environment."[57]

As Mukangoga described her company's work to me, she quickly moved to the topic of empowerment, the first of Haute Baso's three stated values:

Many come out of vocational training in Rwanda, but they are not necessarily equipped to do high-quality work. They need more training, and we are providing them with that.

Training in the trade is not enough, though. It must be more holistic. We care about where they are staying, what's happening at home. If the girls are not fully present [at work], it affects how you're training them. We do a lot more with healthcare. All treatment is free, and we pay for transportation.

MAJORITY WORLD DEFINITION OF THE PROBLEM

Haute Baso is, in my research, a typical example of a Majority World social enterprise. As the owners defined it, the problem to be addressed includes a lack of dignity, power, and hope, and for that reason, they focused their solution on empowerment from the start. I heard this problem and solution repeatedly articulated by Majority World leaders.

Florence Muindi, M.D., M.P.H., is a Kenyan leader of an NGO that now spans fourteen countries on two continents. She explained her perspective this way:

> Capacity among nationals is already there. Building confidence and dignity, doing it *with* rather than *for* them and not by doing it *to* them, training so they can train others—that's our role. Don't be content with just giving services to them. Empower people in the community to give the services themselves.

Jeanine Solo, a Burundian who returned to her home country after living in Uganda for ten years offered,

> I came so that I could make a difference in our community. People are very intelligent, but they lack the skills that can help them come out of their poverty. The women here in Burundi are really suffering and do not know what they can do to meet their needs.

A Filipino leader of an NGO spoke poignantly of a much more broadly defined problem than Americans often conceptualize:

> Even in asking what kind of program to use, you're asking for metrics. It's difficult because you destroy the integrity of a person's life when you want to change them overnight. Will you have the same set of outcomes for

your own children? Integrity of process is destroyed from lack of understanding that it takes time for development to happen.

A lack of power and hope that can be addressed through capacity- and vision-building. This definition of the problem focuses on developing individuals who can then provide for themselves rather than directly addressing their lack of material resources. People from the Majority World with whom I spoke repeatedly expressed their belief that, with the appropriate support, people can and will change their circumstances.

This problem definition reflects how people living in poverty have described their circumstances, as the World Bank global study *Consultations with the Poor* illustrates:

> The rich is the one who says, "I am going to do it" and does it. The poor, in contrast, do not fulfill their wishes or develop their capacities. (Brazilian)
> [Poverty is] like living in jail, living under bondage, waiting to be free. (Jamaican)
> A better life for me is to be healthy, peaceful, and to live in love without hunger. Love is more than anything. Money has no value in the absence of love. (Ethiopian)[58]

Harrison Ngota Airo offered the following description of the complex context in which Kenya's most vulnerable live:

> The Northeastern province, where I worked as a police officer for three years, is … the traditional homeland of the pastoral nomads. Although livestock remains the main source of food and income, it is increasingly unsustainable as the severity of droughts escalates due to climate change … Armed violence is increasing across the district as ethnic tribes clash over limited natural resources.

As the men range farther and longer in search of limited grazing terrain or move to urban slums in search of unskilled labor, the women are left behind in the villages, often without food or income. During times of drought and hunger, they are forced to rely upon emergency food aid, which reinforces the cycle of dependency.

When you move around the villages, the predominant stories are usually around how the world has changed, how things are not easy now. There are increased cases of divorce and separation and conflict within families. The conversations around these issues give birth to anger, frustration, and stigma. People are facing depression, conflict, and envy, and children are at risk of abandonment.

Ngoto describes a complex web of problems highlighting core issues of hopelessness and powerlessness. These are the problems many of the Majority World entrepreneurs I interviewed are working to address.

MAJORITY WORLD EVALUATION

As described previously, American research and evaluation has often reflected Americans' focus on material problems. Majority World entrepreneurs in this study, while not minimizing the devastating consequences of material poverty, tended to emphasize empowerment and evaluated their work based on a broader range of outcomes. For example, Mukangoga of Haute Baso related, "We have a lot of follow up. We are doing a lot of evaluation now. Are they referring anyone to work with us? We assume that means they like working here. How is their family life?"

Global Mamas is a Ghanaian social enterprise that works with female entrepreneurs as they grow their businesses. They provide vocational training as well as training on topics the women request, such as English language skills and personal health. (This enterprise will be discussed in detail in Chapter 18.) Their regular evaluations include "keep[ing] track of trainings, what they have accomplished learning this year. We gather data and look at other things like how many children are going to school or college."

This broader evaluative focus is evident at the professional association level as well. It is noteworthy that the first Implementation Principle of the African Evaluation Association emphasizes empowerment:

> Engage stakeholders in the evaluation process in a manner that facilitates self-discovery and learning, develops accountability, builds capacity in evaluative thinking, and gives life to the notion of self-determination and "nothing about us, without us." Where possible, while maintaining the integrity of the evaluation, co-create the evaluation approach. To the extent that it is feasible and useful, engage with stakeholders about pre-final findings, and consider their perspectives and any supplementary evidence.[59]

How many Americans recognize this deep desire to empower vulnerable people that drives many Majority World leaders? If Americans' focus is on addressing material needs—clean water, agricultural tools—building an enterprise can largely occur at a distance from the target population. There is no need to listen for whether the enterprise's vision and mission are truly valued and embraced by the intended recipients. Culturally, Americans are accustomed to operating as individuals rather than as part of a collective, they do not naturally look for contextual, nonverbal clues that people may be providing, and they operate at a very fast pace. Combine these cultural norms with common American approaches to launching a social enterprise and it becomes easy to see how Americans could easily overlook fundamental differences in goals.

The next chapter looks more deeply at the concept of empowerment and how Majority World leaders in this study worked to create environments in which vulnerable people could experience increased dignity and agency.

PERSPECTIVES

Which do you believe is the most important suffering to address first: physical suffering or a lack of hope and personal dignity? Why?

What assumptions might influence your answer to this question?

How may Americans' emphasis on consumerism influence our definition of the problem that most needs to be solved in other societies as well as our own?

Nine

Increasing Others' Power

"We are sun and moon, dear friend; we are sea and land.
It is not our purpose to become each other; it is to recognize
each other, to learn to see the other, and honor him for what he is:
each the other's opposite and complement."

Hermann Hesse

Sharing power. Creating power. As I spoke with Majority World leaders, many emphasized the importance of empowering vulnerable people rather than simply addressing their material needs. They often defined empowerment in terms of helping individuals and communities build hope, nurturing trust with individuals and community leaders, and displaying respect for those they were trying to help. They had observed that hope, trust, and respect were often lacking in vulnerable people's lives and believed these elements were crucial for sustainable change to occur. This chapter unpacks these elements one at a time.

THE POWER OF HOPE

Majority World leaders I interviewed first expressed concern about the lack of hope they saw among the most vulnerable. Sifuna Wanyonyi of Kenya shared,

> I do pastoral work and also do community social work and counseling…. Where I live, we have about 75 percent of people living for less than a half dollar for a day. They've lost hope in life.

Dr. Sam Adeyemi, senior pastor of the 22,000-member Daystar Christian Centre in Nigeria, also observed limited hope:

> Real and sustainable change in people's lives begins with a change in their sense of identity. People are plagued with self-doubt. Those who have dealt with colonialization tend to have lower self-esteem and very limited vision for what they could be.[60]

Finally, Stanford Chabaya, a social entrepreneur from Zimbabwe, spoke of hope's power:

> In Adana [a mining community], if I marry, my child will also end up working at the mine where I work. That's how people see life. To change this mindset, you must have people see the other side. If they see things differently, they will begin pushing themselves. Change must be a burning desire from within themselves.

Economic research on international development has historically focused almost exclusively on removing barriers to a better life, barriers such as limited or no access to credit, education, or health services.[61] There is now, however, also a growing understanding among Western researchers of the powerful role that hope in particular plays in development efforts.[62, 63] Hope, it is proposed, has three components—having some kind of goal, seeing a pathway to achieve the goal, and believing you can make progress along that pathway.[64] Past research supports hope's important role. It is a key component of resilience in the face of negative shocks,[65] and it is strongly associated with general mental wellness.[66]

Research and the experience of Majority World leaders indicate that hope indeed plays a central role in successful change efforts. Hope builds resilience. Hope offers an achievable vision for the future. Clean water, safe lighting—these additions may not be enough to improve life if vulnerable people are not also empowered through increased hope.

THE POWER OF BUILDING TRUST

Building trust with customers, employees, and community leaders was a second key component of empowerment that Majority World leaders emphasized during my interviews with them. Many were willing to spend significant time and effort to do so. Laud Basing, a Ghanaian microbiologist who leads a medical laboratory service social enterprise, spoke about the essential role of trust and the patience that is often required to build it—even as he worked with fellow Ghanaians as a member of the World Health Organization (WHO):

> There's a conspiracy theory in African countries related to vaccines—the African population is growing, and the West would like to kill a lot of people. If we must take something into our mouths, people associate that something with White people—vaccines, water, certain types of food. They push back.
>
> We were supposed to give them drugs and no one was taking them. We need to see the chief, we decided. The [WHO] leaders said, "No, the chief will not be able to do anything."

We took four opinion leaders to lunch. We didn't start by telling them what we wanted. We asked them about what they needed. We asked them how we should go about achieving our goal of distributing drugs. They said, "No problem. We will get them to do it tomorrow."

Trust. It is an essential ingredient of healthy relationships and, according to John Gottman, a respected researcher on relationships, "Trust is central to what makes human communities work."[67] But while trust plays a significant role in relationships, building trust across cultures can be difficult. One aspect of this challenge is the different role trust plays across societies. For example, David De Cramer, a member of the faculty at the University of Cambridge, observed this about Westerners:

> Generally speaking, in the West, the default is "trust." I'll give you the benefit of the doubt and consider you basically trustworthy until you do something that breaks our trust....
>
> People are used to doing business almost immediately when they work in the same industry. Westerners feel more comfortable conducting business and building trust at the same time if the opportunity arises.[68]

The Majority World leaders I interviewed, on the other hand, often took a time-intensive approach to build trust at the beginning of a relationship. They engaged in extended conversations with potential customers and employees and with community leaders. They also simply spent time with people as relationships began.

A young Zimbabwean working with a British NGO reflected on the tension he felt as he acknowledged the time required to build trust in his culture:

> I would get really frustrated because people in the villages we were trying to help did not want the help. They wanted

me to go to a cave, drink beer, do all kinds of things to get the village leaders to agree to do this. I'm like, "I'm leaving. I'll go somewhere that wants us." But I should be more motivated to help them even with these requirements.

Trust is essential to healthy relationships and is also directly related to empowerment. Research on the American workplace has found employees who feel the most empowered in their work environment also tend to have the highest levels of trust in their managers.[69] Similarly, research with Canadian nurses found that those who felt most empowered reported the highest levels of trust in the organization.[70]

This cultural difference in building trust can prove difficult for Americans. Spending time at the beginning of a business relationship simply getting to know each other and building trust is not an American value. It goes against our need to use time carefully and sparingly. It goes against our natural bent toward building trust as the business moves forward and assuming trustworthiness until proven otherwise. It also goes against our tendency to focus on individuals rather than whole communities and particularly community leaders. These different approaches can unfortunately lead to significant distrust of Americans and can work against empowerment of the vulnerable people they are intending to serve.

THE POWER OF RESPECT

Finally, Majority World leaders emphasized the need to create relationships based on mutual respect. Stanford Chabaya from Zimbabwe explained,

Cultivate the right frame of mind. People want to exploit opportunities. Having done that, people don't always want to be assisted. They appreciate the scenario where something is set up so they can do something for themselves. They want to be able to do things after the assistance has come through and left.

Dr. George, who leads Life Medical Services (Chapter 3), operationalized his desire to convey respect to patients this way, "We ensure employment of other medical workers in such a way that a patient is able to get the right medical attention the minute they walk into the hospital."

Others with whom I spoke built training programs around employees' priorities and allowed employees to set their work hours around the demands of their farms as concrete means of conveying respect.

Respect, which can be defined as "the basic human valuing of people for who they are and for what they uniquely contribute to [a group],"[71] is crucial because of the central role it plays in building healthy relationships. Each of us is motivated in part by a need to experience respect from others.[72] Indeed an American study has found that respect from friends and co-workers was significantly related to people's overall sense of well-being while, interestingly enough, socioeconomic status was not.[73]

Economists studying the value of various approaches for addressing poverty are beginning to explore respect's role. Based on a study that involved six countries on three continents, Nobel prize-winning researchers suggested,

> But perhaps we need to go beyond these standard theories.... Perhaps this program worked by making beneficiaries feel that they mattered, that the rest of society cared about them, that with this initial help they now had some control over their future well-being, and therefore, the future could become better.[74]

As with hope and trust, Majority World leaders I interviewed believed there is power that comes from feeling respected. They were therefore willing to invest time in building relationships with customers and employees that were founded upon respect for their values and lifestyles.

AMERICANS AND EMPOWERMENT

Helping people find hope can create new power. Building trust-based relationships and conveying respect can require transferring some of one's power. This is time-consuming, and at times humbling work, but it is work that Majority World leaders view as essential.

Americans working in international development, however, may not view themselves as having strong relational skills or the necessary time to empower people by nurturing trust, hope, and mutual respect. It is easier to keep moving forward with plans, with our natural approach to solving the problem we have identified. But what is the danger of holding significant power while investing little time in empowering others? Several I interviewed spoke to this question, including Ghanaian social entrepreneur Marigold Adu:

Unfortunately, you have many Americans who think they know the world, but their life is concentrated on the U.S. of A. Americans have diversity—geographic, racial. There's no reason to travel anywhere. If you want to experience a hot climate, you go to Florida. Unfortunately, there is a superiority complex that's instilled, a "Mr. America" complex. When they come in, they have the answers. They come to do what Superman would do. It becomes difficult to even have a conversation …

Americans want it the way they've always had it. "It's so hot. There are so many mosquitos." When a Chinese man comes … It's hot. Okay, he takes his shirt off, wears a hat, fans himself. He's on-site and he's ready to talk contract. The American? He is talking about when he next gets on a plane. It makes you feel he's not interested in a relationship.

How can you work through others? How can you not be seen but work through others? Americans don't want to pay the price because not everyone will jump at your idea.

Joachim Ewechu, co-founder and CEO of SHONA, also commented on Americans' limited proximity to people and the message this conveys:

There are two kinds of expats living here. I am not a fan of one type—the type that comes in to work with a big MNC [multinational corporation]. They live on a hill with big SUVs. I don't know how much progress they make. I don't know how they get to know what they need to learn by not living on the ground. You need to have a love for the local people. Look at them as people, as human beings. Have conversations with them and treat them as normal friends. They think they know everything, but they don't know anything.

Finally, Roland Hoksbergen, an American economics professor who married a Guatemalan woman and lived for years in Latin America, expressed concern about Americans' lack of focus on empowerment:

Businesspeople want to come in with a business solution … Those who are successful are those who bridge both worlds—the historical, contextual, cultural, as well as the business side. American businesses seem to let the bottom-line dictate their timeline while developing countries seem to base their business partnerships on relationships and dependability that can only be built with time.

The next chapter continues to wrestle with the topic of empowerment and the dangers associated with power. It explores key assumptions many Americans I interviewed seemed to operate under and Majority World responses to these assumptions.

PERSPECTIVES

Encouraging locals' dependency on Americans is a danger that must be avoided, even if the enterprise must grow at a slower pace than anticipated.

Under what circumstances do you agree with this statement? Are there circumstances when allowing dependency for a limited time is acceptable to bring about an important change?

Describe a time when you felt particularly empowered. What factors contributed to that feeling? Describe a time when you felt particularly disempowered. What factors contributed to that feeling? Which of the factors you identified are likely culture-specific and which are likely universal?

Ten

Assumptions

"Perhaps the most critical point—and the one hardest to keep clearly in mind—is that help is always defined by the recipient. Taking an action with respect to someone because 'it is best for him …' may be influencing him, but it is not providing help unless he so perceives it."

Douglas McGregor

Melinda French Gates was interviewed about her role as a philanthropist. She shared about the universal desire to give our children good things such as education and health care and to be able to time pregnancies so that we can give these things to each of our children. She then described the end of her conversation with a woman she had met in the slums of Nairobi:

[This woman] finally summed it up. "I want to give every single good thing to this child." And she was holding this little baby girl. "I want to give every single good thing to her before I have another child." I thought, "This woman is summing up our work in the world." We all as parents want to give every good thing to our children. There's something that we ought to be able to do about that.[75]

Her comment made me wonder. What is "every good thing" that we parents want to give our children? Is this defined the same around the world or does the list of "good things" differ by culture? Often our assumptions are hidden, but they directly drive our vision for a flourishing world. We must recognize, and if necessary, challenge our assumptions if we are to engage more effectively with people across cultures.

As described in Chapter 8, the American and Majority World leaders I interviewed generally defined the problem to be solved in different ways. Not surprisingly, their underlying assumptions seemed to differ as well. On the following page is a table highlighting assumptions that many I interviewed expressed. Some assumptions were explicitly stated while others were conveyed through the stories they shared with me.

The remainder of this chapter unpacks these differing assumptions one by one, using the common American assumption as the starting point. The first assumption, about problem definition, was explored in depth in Chapter 8.

AMERICAN ASSUMPTION #2
WE ALL SHARE A COMMON DEFINITION OF
AN ACCEPTABLE STANDARD OF LIVING

The definition of an acceptable standard of living, it turns out, depends on who you ask. An American's definition would most likely include clean water nearby, a latrine, and electricity. It is a list that reflects our cultural values. For example, Americans value efficiency because time is a precious, finite commodity to us. Walking two hours each day for clean water would be irrational.

Assumptions

American	Majority World
1. We all agree on the problem to be solved.	1. Americans often define a highly focused problem rather than the larger challenge of empowering people and communities to address problems themselves.
2. We all share a common definition of an acceptable standard of living.	2. The definition of an acceptable standard of living is culture-specific.
3. A satisfying life is defined essentially the same in every culture; most people aspire to the American way of life.	3. Definitions of a satisfying life differ; embracing American culture could be destructive to our society.
4. Americans, on their own, possess solutions to the problems of poverty in the Majority World.	4. The priorities and assets of people from the Majority World must be part of any development strategy; there is tremendous power found in helping one's own community.
5. Americans are generally viewed as trustworthy in the Majority World; historical friction between the U.S. and a Majority World country is not relevant to my work.	5. Americans, regardless of their role and perspective, are more similar than different from each other; historically, they have often been driven by selfish motives so each person must prove their trustworthiness.
6. Little personal vulnerability is needed to build a sustainable and effective enterprise.	6. Building trust and hope and conveying respect to those with whom you work is essential; this requires vulnerability.

Americans also place a high value on achievement and productivity:

- A Gallup poll found our average workweek is now forty-three hours.[76]
- Forty percent of Americans get less than the recommended seven hours of sleep per night.[77]
- Employees had an average of 9.5 unused vacation days in 2021.[78]

Given this emphasis on achievement, investing in tools such as electricity to increase our productivity is an obvious choice. However, American views of what is essential do not necessarily match the views of those from the Majority World.

Regarding water, Laud Basing, a Ghanaian entrepreneur shared,

> I know of a small town where the women have to walk two towns away to fetch water. Americans built a boondoggle. They had a big ceremony when it was finished. Women bypassed it and continued to walk to the water two towns away. What outsiders didn't understand is that this was their break. They were able to talk, socialize. The well was cutting into their social life.

Marigold Adu, a fellow Ghanaian, was part of this conversation and added,

> They are not interested in the well because you are actually causing problems for them. It causes depression, loneliness, fatigue. There is social disease because of the well. [Walking two towns away to get water, and talking along the way, means] you have a happy home, a happy family. She has a distressing area in her life, and she goes back to her husband with no problems after going to get water.

Regarding latrines, a Zambian entrepreneur shared, "I enjoy the walk into the bush. It is relaxing."

Regarding electricity, Adu observed,

We are happy without electricity. A person goes to his farm when the sun comes up. He rests at 6 o'clock when the sun goes down. He has no desire to connect to the internet. He does not need electricity.... God gave me wiry hair. I don't need to blow dry it or straighten it. Why do I need electricity?

Would Americans go to an Amish community and try to sell them light bulbs? No. They are happy with their lives the way they are. Why do Americans come to Africa trying to do the same thing?

I am not suggesting that no one in the Majority World wants clean water nearby or electricity. However, I repeatedly heard that there are often bigger dreams at play—dreams such as increased dignity and hope and utilizing local resources to build a more secure future for oneself and one's community. When American initiatives put those priorities at risk, there will be push back.

AMERICAN ASSUMPTION #3
THE DEFINITION OF A SATISFYING LIFE IS ESSENTIALLY THE SAME IN EVERY CULTURE

For many Americans, living the American Dream entails financial security and hopefully prosperity. Generally, we assume that possessing ample money is an essential component of a satisfying life. But as I listened, I heard alternate forms of prosperity described during the interviews—prosperity in terms of relationships, contentment, and respect. For many people, these forms of prosperity are more highly prized than material wealth.

Prospering in Relationships

Stephen Eyman, an American who married a Guatemalan and has lived for years in rural parts of Latin America, observed the following:

> So many acts of generosity. Giving something that isn't just your surplus but that is vital to your needs. Food that you need but you give to someone else anyway. They feel like they want to do something for you. They just do it regardless of what it means for them later.
>
> Everyone ends up living with a better quality of life because of sharing money when one or another has it. Money comes and goes but you feel secure in your finances because you have so many friendships and relationships.
>
> I lived in one of the poorest regions in Colombia but for that reason, people were much more willing to help each other out, especially with things that involve fun. You pay for each other.
>
> "I have no money." "Come and we'll see how to make it work." If you show up at someone's house at mealtime, they don't make more. They just divide it up among more people.

Prospering in Contentment

Junior Auguistin, a Haitian who co-leads an adventure-tourism social enterprise for Westerners, also spoke about an alternate form of prosperity—prosperity through contentment:

> I know in the West people really want to have more and more. So here you can see some people with nothing, but they always smile, they are always happy. But in the U.S., you have the thing you call "time is money." Everything you do really quickly because you should go back to work.

I asked Auguistin why he believes many Haitians are always happy.

> For me, where we grew up, the situation didn't work well. We always fought with life. So, you have an obligation to be happy because you're not thinking about big money. You're not thinking, "Tomorrow we are going to have a lot of money." Everything you have in your hand, you are happy with it. You eat rice, you are happy with it.
>
> The difference I can see for other countries like yours— as children grow up, they see the country has jobs, people keep pushing to have more and more. So, as people grow up, they have an obligation to enter this competition, to keep moving to have more and more.

Prospering in Respect

People also spoke about prosperity through respect. Valerie, a social entrepreneur in Haiti, talked with local women who were artisans. She asked them what they valued about their business. "The first thing they mentioned was respect. They got much more respect from their husbands, children, and from the community because they were generating an income and selling things in the marketplace."

Valerie shared the story of Nicole, a Haitian artisan:

> She was poor, but she understood how to look at things and make money with them. She had three daughters and only sent one to school. She heard about a solar oven via a seminar and then took a loan from us, leveraged her employment with us, and paid it back. She bought two. She used them to make bread samples and took them to churches. She made bread as her new business.
>
> She used the oven to create a business for herself. She has made chocolate bars, hair oil, all with the oven. She

put herself into professional school. Wow, this woman in a male-dominated society! She would give her neighbors small interest-free loans, use the ovens to cook their beans, sponsor other kids in her zone to go to school. She became an elder, a really respected member of society because of the business. Especially in a male-dominated society, she stood out.

Nicole looks like the same woman who walked in years ago. Her own standard of living looks the same, but she constantly talks about the respect she has, that now she is an elder.

Just as Majority World villagers do not outright reject clean water, electricity, and latrines but at times determine that the benefits are not worth the cost, so it is with material prosperity. Most individuals from the Majority World would welcome additional material resources. However, many view intangibles such as relationships, contentment, and respect as more important contributions than physical resources to a satisfying life. These three currencies speak again to the importance individuals around the world assign to feeling empowered.

AMERICAN ASSUMPTION #4
AMERICANS, ON THEIR OWN, POSSESS SOLUTIONS TO THE PROBLEMS OF POVERTY IN THE MAJORITY WORLD

By virtue of independently building a social enterprise in a Majority World country, many of the Americans I interviewed seem to agree with this assumption. Throughout the interviews, however, Majority World leaders expressed varying forms of frustration with this approach. Following is a brief sample of what I heard.

Mavis Thandizo Kanjadza from Malawi observed,

One-third of Malawi is a lake. We shouldn't be dealing with drought. We have water.... When you tell us that we should build our economy on our own, but money keeps coming, I feel like it is doing us a disservice.

If we were cornered to make things work, it would be better. I feel like we are overgrown children staying with their parents. I'll have food, I want pizza. We are over-reliant. We have many resources. Tourism should be booming, but it's not. We have the best weather and this lake that is beautiful.

We have two Americans who have come. They started a company, Malawi Mangos. They grow them and sell them. Did we need them to do this? No. It will be hard when the aid is pulled out. But if we don't go through this pain, we might be like this indefinitely.

Joachim Ewechu, co-founder and CEO of SHONA commented,

It should be a 50/50 partnership. They bring in the future for us, we bring the local context. Together we make a formidable team. Americans need to respect what we bring as well. We're partners. Empower us by respecting who we are. We need you to look at us as valuable human beings who can bring important things to the table.

Finally, Oscar Muriu, senior pastor of Nairobi Chapel, remarked,

One exchange that takes place in a true partnership is a transfer of power. It empowers the non-dominant culture and disempowers the dominant culture.... Trust allows the partnership to move forward, but sometimes we don't build into trust enough.

We see it differently in the South than the North. It's a relationship that recognizes we're interdependent upon one another. Problems come when one form of equity is valued over another form of equity. Every partnership must build reciprocity. When you don't allow reciprocity, you end up with the dreaded monster of dependency.

You must empower the Southern Hemisphere to recognize it too has something to give, because there is honor then in receiving your gift if we have something else to give back in return ... You need us whether you know it or not.

Equalized power. Unique assets that those from the Majority World must contribute if initiatives are to bring about lasting, positive change. These are themes I heard repeatedly during interviews with Majority World leaders and themes that will be explored more deeply in later chapters.

AMERICAN ASSUMPTION #5
AMERICANS ARE GENERALLY VIEWED AS
TRUSTWORTHY IN THE MAJORITY WORLD

A few of the Americans in this study articulated the value of establishing trust with those they were trying to help. Jennifer, who imports fair trade products into the U.S., shared this story:

The biggest help is when someone local can vouch for me. This happened with one gentleman in Kenya, Simon, who is now my most trusted client. When I would go and visit a community or group, he would come with me and say things like, "She is good. Keep doing what she is asking you to do." It built trust. Now he has built an extra room in his house for me to stay when I come.

However, no American I interviewed offered that Americans generally have a trust deficit in the Majority World. On the other hand, I did hear this concern articulated by many Majority World leaders. For example, a man from Ethiopia offered,

> People of the world do not think that America wants to help. We have heard many stories and we've seen many things and many damages done by America. Americans may want to help, but from our perspective, that is not the case.
>
> Americans advance their own interests. They don't care about others. They don't care about the dignity of the human being. America must understand the culture of the people they want to help. You can't help if you define the problem your way. You must understand the culture and the needs as we say them.

A man from Namibia articulated the sentiment this way:

> The ruthlessness of the American/European market. I constantly tell people that if you want Africa to go forward, stop colonizing Africa. Everybody wants to be the Good Samaritan. I don't think Africa needs saving. Every other country is protecting its interests. The longer it takes us to rise, the longer you can stay on top. Namibia is the world's largest uranium producer. We also produce lots of beef and diamonds. We should be able to support ourselves.

The implications of different assumptions regarding Americans' trustworthiness can be significant when building partnerships across cultures, to say the least.

AMERICAN ASSUMPTION #6
LITTLE PERSONAL VULNERABILITY IS NEEDED
TO BUILD A SUSTAINABLE AND EFFECTIVE ENTERPRISE

A sixth assumption conveyed in the interviews revolved around the role of personal vulnerability in building an enterprise. It was uncommon for the Americans I interviewed to prioritize this as they worked. Their focus was most often on how to get the operation up and running and then to keep it running.

Bryan Stevenson, founder and Executive Director of the Equal Justice Initiative in Montgomery, Alabama, believes emotional and physical distance is characteristic of Americans' approach to local challenges as well:

> To change the world, to create justice, to do difficult things, we have got to get proximate to the people who are suffering, who we are serving. We cannot be effective leaders from a distance … I am persuaded that most of us live in communities where we have been taught that if there is a bad part of town where there is a lot of violence or abuse or neglect or despair, most of us have been taught to stay as far away from that part of town as possible … I think there is power in proximity.[79]

Many Majority World social entrepreneurs, on the other hand, shared with me how they had intentionally gotten proximate and even humbled themselves in a desire to empower others. Dr. George with Life Medical Services said, "We believe that patients are our bosses. That is different from the cultural phenomenon. We need to give them a service. Without them we would not have a hospital" (Chapter 3). Mavis Thandizo Kanjadza shared a specific example of humbling herself to empower farmers:

> I was new to farming and everyone's farm looked perfect on Facebook. Every time I went to my farm I was

depressed. My farm doesn't look like that. My onions didn't look perfect but every other person's onions looked perfect on Facebook.

I brought my onions to an extension person. "These don't look right," I said. The extension person said, "They look fine. This is how onions grow." I remember this guy telling me that this is the journey he'd gone through. He was vulnerable. "Don't stop within the first three years," he told me. He gave me books to read.

That's when I looked back. I had bought into the lie of social media. I was keeping up appearances with someone's highlights. That's when I realized we can use social media to help people who are entrepreneurs. I can be vulnerable on social media to help others.

CONCLUSION

In this study, Americans' assumptions were often quite different from those held by people from the Majority World. However, factors such as physical distance, optimism, a fast pace, and a belief that people around the world share similar aspirations keep many Americans unaware of these foundational differences. Americans' unrecognized assumptions may also stem from their strong desire to share their good fortune or blessings with others. According to some I interviewed, guilt can be a motivating factor for social entrepreneurs, especially those who have amassed significant wealth. The more I have, the thinking goes, the more responsibility I bear to make sure those less fortunate also have adequate resources. But people in the Majority World do not necessarily see themselves as living in need of this type of "blessing." Instead, they want opportunities to increase their agency and dignity.

It is uncommon for a person to recognize the assumptions that were presented in this chapter, much less question their accuracy. Nevertheless, these assumptions can markedly shape the enterprise we attempt to build. When different sets of assumptions collide, friction ensues. This friction and its related power struggles are the focus of the next chapter.

PERSPECTIVES

This chapter described several assumptions Americans may hold. Which assumption do you believe is most common? Which do you believe is least common?

Why do you believe Americans tend to remain emotionally and sometimes physically distant from the people they are trying to help? What do Americans forfeit if they do not get proximate?

Eleven

Points of Friction

"For good ideas and true innovation,
you need human interaction, conflict, argument, debate."

Margaret Heffernan

Given different cultural norms, different definitions of the problem to be solved, and different assumptions, it is not surprising that stories about friction came up repeatedly in the interviews for this study. This chapter explores seven common areas of friction that people identified during the interviews and relies heavily on interviewees' voices to describe them.

1. THE PACE OF WORK AND ENTERPRISE EXPANSION

The first common frustration I heard revolved around perceptions of the pace at which things should move, which is logical given significant cultural differences about the nature of time. Excerpts from an American social entrepreneur's notes as he built a business capture his frustration:

> Many delays. Hard to put on the pressure or understand what the real delays are.
>
> DR Congo site is still not open. Every week they say next week it will happen. This has been going on for two months. Our conclusions about "readiness"—the locals tend not to plan but count on being able to work around problems only when they must. The forcing function is our presence, unfortunately.

James Owolabi, a Nigerian who has lived for two decades in the United States, observed this about Americans and time:

> When you give an American a project, they are not going to take no for an answer. They get it done. That's what's beautiful about Americans. Hispanic people take naps. The British have a teatime. Americans? They invented the whole night shift concept. We [Africans] don't have that. Americans don't value rest. They stick to things. They get them done.

Frustration with different approaches to time can quickly become palpable for Majority World people as well. Comments I heard ranged from gentle advice to heartfelt discouragement over Westerners' push to accomplish change in a short amount of time.

Daliso Chitundu, a Zambian social entrepreneur, described the friction this way, "Americans have a lack of patience. In our culture, we like to stroll, not walk."

As we talked about our different time perspectives, a social entrepreneur from India laughed and said, "Hurry, hurry doesn't go over well in India." A Filipino leader of an NGO described the frustration this way. "The people in the West have watches, but they don't have time. In our region, we don't have a watch, but we make time. The difficulty is that you're always in a hurry to look for results. Transformation can never be done overnight."

Stephen Eyman is an American, married to a Guatemalan, who has spent years living in Central and South America. As someone who has developed an understanding of American culture as well as several Latin American cultures, his insight is especially valuable. He contrasted Latin American and American time perspectives this way:

Americans often think you can accomplish something in a three-day window. We had a meeting scheduled in the mountains, and it's a two-hour ride in a jeep to get there. But the rain came, and no Colombian was there for the meeting. It's a desert, a savannah. Americans thought it was laziness, but the main transportation is motorcycle taxi, not car taxi. That's too expensive, and no one wants to ride a motorcycle taxi in the rain because it's not safe, and they don't want to get wet. The Colombians just said, "We can figure it out later. People have to be flexible."

How could you expect someone to get up the mountain in a specific period of time? You could have to walk or take a donkey because the road had caved in. Then we [Americans] assume Colombians are lazy. They take a 12:00 to 2:00 rest. But what we don't understand is that they get up at 5:00 a.m. to work. They work six hours before their siesta, and we assume they didn't work much. Then they work more after their siesta.

I worked with a guy who would always say, "Give it more *suave.*" A little slower. Be relaxed. Let the weight of it fall. If you work too hard, you will wear out. You can only last a few hours like that when out in 100-degree weather. This guy gets up early; he's out there for a long time. He's able to do that for sixty years straight. His body never gives out. Amazing what he can accomplish in a lifetime. Food is always there. Work gets done. It's just a matter of pacing yourself.

Radically different views of time cause friction. Different definitions of the problem only add to that friction. If the goal is to get essential material resources to as many people as possible, time is of the essence, as Americans' pace reflects. But if the goal is to support people as they transform their lives, the amount of time needed becomes almost irrelevant. Moving at a fast pace may further disempower people if they do not feel they are partners in the quest for a solution. This brings us to a second common source of friction.

2. THE NATURE OF BUSINESS RELATIONSHIPS

Several people interviewed for this study described differences in how American and Majority World leaders view business relationships. If the goal is to increase people's access to key material resources, business relationships are logically just that—business-focused, goal-oriented relationships without significant personal ties. Culturally, this is Americans' typical way of operating.

I attended a USAID-sponsored panel specifically focused on food-related partnerships that illustrated Americans' common approach. One panel member represented an American food innovation lab. When specifically asked to speak about her organization's partnerships, the woman said,

"We do not have the capacity to disseminate the technology we develop. We must have partners for this. We must also have funding partners."

Rather than forming partnerships with key people and organizations who could bring valuable perspectives and knowledge to the food innovation lab, she described businesses with whom they contracted strictly to distribute their technologies or fund their work.

The next American panelist, a leader in a major agricultural company, did not even mention partnerships when he spoke. Although specifically asked to talk about partnerships, he instead described how his company sold its products in the Majority World and why it is not tremendously profitable to do so. For many Americans, substantive, long-term partnerships, particularly across cultures, are simply not an option they consider.

In many Majority World countries, on the other hand, partnerships are defined by very different cultural norms. Oscar Muriu, senior pastor of Nairobi Chapel, spoke at a gathering I attended. He captured reasons for the tension around these differing concepts of partnership:

> When we talk about partnerships today, two major models resonate with us. Often those from the Northern Hemisphere define partnerships around a business model—mergers, incorporating together, collaborating, getting a task done with a timeline on it and a budget attached to it.
>
> We talk about partnership like a marriage. There is courting, there is a commitment, and a covenant. There is longevity to the relationship—until death do us part. When we in the Southern Hemisphere have a significant partner, we name our children after that partner.
>
> When we work with these two different models, we wonder why there are issues of trust, why partnerships bring so much hurt in the relationship, why partners disappear. The task is done, and the partnership is done, those from the North think. We wonder why people disappear when the work is over. We feel divorced.

Individualism and collectivism, masculine and feminine approaches to building an enterprise, high versus low context cultures, urgency versus a long-term view—numerous differences contribute to friction around the nature of business relationships.

3. THE PRIMACY OF INNOVATION VS. RESTORATION

A third area of friction that came up multiple times in the interviews reflects a tension between the value of an innovation developed by an outside party and the value of restoration. Before I share comments made by those I interviewed, let's look at the role that innovation plays in the United States.

Americans love thinking outside the box, and we prize innovators such as Steve Jobs and Elon Musk. We also value creativity. In terms of movies, it is interesting to note that all fifteen movies with the highest global box office revenue are American produced.[80] Looking at another form of creativity, Nobel prizes are awarded each year to those who "have conferred the greatest benefit to humankind" in the fields of physics, chemistry, medicine, literature, and peace.[81] The United States has only 4 percent of the world's population, but our multinational population includes 34 percent of its Nobel laureates.[82]

Americans value innovation and creativity, and these values naturally carry over to the creative ways in which we approach problems facing people in the Majority World. But because Americans generally prefer to operate alone rather than in partnership with local people, innovations are typically developed apart from the intended users.

Gary Burniske, an American who lived in South America and Central Asia for more than twenty years, offered commentary about the friction that can accompany this approach:

> People are under the assumption regarding small landholder families who are living on the edge that they have plenty of time to spare. People living on the edge are often the busiest, so acceptance of new technologies and new techniques that require a time investment are hard to meet.
>
> People are promoting soil conservation—keep your crop from blowing away, increase productivity. It's a no-

brainer from a Westerner's perspective. But if you aren't in your fields or selling something or busy trying to find your next meal doing odds and ends to have cash to buy food … that becomes the reason there is a push back on adopting a newly introduced technology.

Short trips by faculty who work and study only in the United States [are a problem]. They have been in a university setting for forty years but have never spent significant time abroad or outside to have that understanding. People are the hardest part of any program. Tech solutions are the easy part.

Burniske is speaking to the reality that innovations generally offer both costs and benefits. The potential benefits are usually obvious, at least to Americans, but the costs are often far less so. An American's perspective may be just the opposite of those to whom the innovation is being marketed. The intended user may readily see the innovation's drawbacks while the benefits are far less clear cut.

On several occasions, I had the privilege of talking with more than one social entrepreneur at a time and was able to learn from their interactions with each other. Especially telling was a conversation between Collins Nyamadzawo, a Zimbabwean, and Marigold Adu, a Ghanaian, as they wrestled with the potential cost of innovations to a culture. Nyamadzawo came from an area where villages could not retain their teachers because they did not have electricity. He approached a British NGO that was willing to bring hydroelectricity to these villages, but he experienced deep frustration because people in the villages were not convinced that they needed the help.

Adu responded,

You have to know that the solution will work, and you have to build trust. You cannot help if you have no trust. You see it as a problem that there are no teachers in the villages. They don't see it as a problem. If you have no teachers, you don't have to send your kids to school, and you can send them instead to the farm. That is good.

So, do you try to do it anyway? When you go in with answers, you find they are not applicable. The syllabus at school, for example, doesn't relate to their lives. British colonization gave us winter, summer, spring, fall. We are going to school during the sessions when we should be growing.

The minute you bring in something from the outside, we ask why. I will be able to feed my country with the skills my parents taught me. It is okay to be on my family's farm part of the time and in school part of the time. I may not get the best grades, I may miss part of the curriculum, but I will learn other things from farming.

Many times, potential customers are not convinced of their need for an American innovation, even if it is something Americans perceive as essential. As Adu observed, "It is a problem if people say it is. Until then, it is not a problem…. The best way to help people is to give them the opportunity to use the wealth they have in their country to make wealth."

Americans' emphasis on externally developed innovations contrasts with an emphasis on restoration that I repeatedly heard as I interviewed social entrepreneurs and other leaders from the Majority World. Most often, their passion was to offer people a better way to use the resources they already had available to them. A social entrepreneur from southern Africa described the tension between innovation and restoration this way:

Conservation farming is what most [foreign] entrepreneurs in [my country] are pushing. They brought a technology which they developed in whatever place and they put it in the fields. It's labor-intensive. It's beautiful. I love it, but it's not practical. And so, what happens is as soon as the field officers turn their backs, the people go to the easier way of doing it. Use the skills I already have and use my basic technology and my basic need to uplift, to make me better.

I heard several examples of this restorative approach as I interviewed Majority World entrepreneurs. Their work often involves using existing local resources in innovative ways or simply using existing local resources more efficiently. Sylvie Sangwa, a Rwandan with a master's degree in agricultural economics, is an example of someone using this approach:

I was in South Africa. I noticed that the richest people are farmers. In my culture, when you say you are from a farming family they say, "Oh, I'm sorry." So I said, "We need some change. If South African people can make a living on agriculture, we can too."

My education includes environmental sustainability. I started a company producing healthy foods using methods that are not harming the environment. I focused on livestock because the land I purchased was not producing after being exhausted.

I started with goats, but that didn't work. I then moved to turkeys and rabbits, then to free range chickens and hogs. The latter did wonders to my poor, exhausted land. Scattered manure on the land coupled with rain revived the place.

Then I introduced fruit trees to exploit all that regained fertility with the vision that the trees would also give back to the animals with the ripened guava fruits falling down and complementing the animals' diet. The trees also provide needed shade because the area is very sunny, and the animals need some protection from the sun. I will not need to fertilize or spray the trees. The animals help with all the bugs that could endanger the trees simply by eating them.

This is a system where everything is sustainably interlinked, each enterprise helping the other in a way that preserves natural resources instead of depleting them; a system that preserves ecosystems and increases biodiversity.

Sangwa has intimate knowledge of her region's local resources and how to use them to bring about a desired change. Many Majority World people I interviewed valued restoration in part because of its ability to empower people and substantially limit the risk of dependency on outsiders. The value that Americans often place on innovation stood at times in stark contrast to this approach, and, not surprisingly, resulted in frustration and misunderstanding across the cultures.

4. THE APPROACH TO INTRODUCING A NEW PRODUCT

A fourth area of related friction stems from the different ways American and Majority World leaders introduce their product or service to potential customers. This friction can stem from different emphases on innovation versus restoration, differences in perceived need, and cultural differences in how new ideas and products are typically marketed in a society.

For Americans with the perspective that their product or service will offer a significant benefit to the consumer, their marketing approach makes sense. Share the idea with as many people as possible as quickly as possible so they can get the product into their hands and see their lives improve.

But this approach does not always work as expected. American-style marketing, which is highly effective in American culture, can be received negatively if people feel pressured to buy something they do not believe they need. This is particularly likely if they perceive they are being demeaned for their current way of life. And thus, a form of power-play ensues.

Introduced in Chapter 3, Bright Lights has tried several marketing approaches—partnering with nonprofits, bringing nationals to the United States to join the team, and hiring nationals to be distributors in their own countries. Despite all of this, Wall has met with only mixed success:

We do have some shining stars [on our sales team], but most aren't doing well. We're having a hard time figuring out how to scale this. It's a very donor-dependent model now … We aren't making it. It's not a runaway success … We definitely have our demons. It's just hard. I don't know why.

We have big plans, big hearts, and empty wallets—just like all social enterprises I know, sadly. But we are figuring it out. The patience game is the hard part as I am impatient.

I asked Laud Basing, a Ghanaian social entrepreneur, why he thought Bright Lights weren't selling. "I've used a lantern for a long time. My parents used it. Nothing has happened."

"No health problems?" I asked. Basing responded,

Right. You come and tell me to use a solar lamp. Why? The best thing he could have done is to go to people in the city. Give a few free samples to people, opinion leaders. There really are opinion leaders.

Generally, people do not like a lot of change. If you want to promote your lamp, promote it as an *addition* to a kerosene lamp. So, when they start using the solar lamp and find it to be better than the kerosene lamp, that will fade out. But if you come attacking the kerosene lamp, what you are telling me is that I'm stupid to be using the kerosene lamp, and therefore, I should use your lamp. I will tell you I am not stupid to part with my money.

Marigold Adu, another Ghanaian social entrepreneur, has also observed resistance to how new ideas are sold by Americans:

> Collaborate with others to create more impact. They will tell others. The approach is where the problem is. Americans discard what we know and bring in what they think they know without even listening.
>
> As human beings, we want to collaborate. Lots of people come with book knowledge rather than practical knowledge. They may only know the theory. For example, you go into a community to solve a housing problem, but the people use thatched roofs. First, you have to understand why thatch works for them. Perhaps it keeps the inside cool when it's hot outside. People are probably migrant people. [Foreigners] want to make them stay, want to build them permanent structures.
>
> That superiority approach. "You are so behind, and you don't know where the world is headed." But some people are quite happy with the lives they live.

Adu has learned to follow this collaborative approach to introducing a new idea as she co-leads Global Bamboo Products Limited, a company that grows and processes bamboo for a variety of purposes:

> When I started managing the factory, I was saying [to a worker] "You have to be there at 7:00." Mom, who co-leads the business, says, "You aren't going to achieve that goal. He will go to his farm by 6:00 a.m. He will come back home and eat what his wife has cooked before he comes to the factory. How are you going to approach that? How will you get him there at 7:00? If you want to be effective, ask him, 'What time can you come? What can you achieve for me today?' Please let him stick to that habit. You will achieve more."

I said, "Show up around 7:00." He showed up around 9:00. He didn't understand the economic benefits to himself. I gave him the job of drying bamboo. "Make it your project," I said. "Charge me for it. I'm giving you the inputs but charge me. Then you will look for workers, for people who can help you do this."

"You know what, Madam? The cost of this thing is more than two month's wages." He still told me he has to go to the farm in the morning. I said, "I'm paying you two month's wages for this," but he was interested in maintaining his lifestyle.

The impact came over time. He realized every day he was working [for us] he would earn what it would take to earn in a month or more as a cocoa farmer. He only got that epiphany at the end. So now when I call him, he's happy to score [bamboo].

Different definitions of the problem that needs to be solved, different views of time, different views of the need to co-labor vs. independently achieve a goal—so many differences contribute to this friction around how best to sell ideas. Adu and Basing described push back when individuals believe outsiders are trying to "fix" them with their product or service. They described the value of proximity rather than distance. They each also mentioned the typical means of introducing a new product in many collectivist cultures—through opinion leaders and word of mouth more generally.

5. THE VALUE OF SCALING

A fifth area of friction that wove through the interviews involved an initiative's scope. Scaling makes perfect sense to many Americans. If I can create a way to provide clean, affordable water for 1,000 people, why would I not rapidly expand to provide clean water for 100,000? And from a financial perspective, if economies of scale exist, an enterprise can achieve greater efficiencies and either improve profit margins or lower prices. These are highly rational goals.

But if the goal is to empower and restore dignity to vulnerable people, then treating them impersonally and focusing on providing for the masses could actually leave people worse off than before the entrepreneur arrived. Several of the Majority World individuals I interviewed spoke about this friction. An Indian social entrepreneur who was trained in the United States offered the following:

> Scaling is seen as critical. But we all [social entrepreneurs] come from a business background. Why is it that scaling is the essential outcome? The ideals of entrepreneurial behavior are very American—it's good to fail, to keep changing. The way Indians look at entrepreneurship is different.
>
> We extol the virtues of an entrepreneur, but we don't stop to ask, are we doing the right thing? Entrepreneurialism in India is not necessarily a virtue.

Mavis Thandizo Kanjadza of Malawi lamented,

> We don't want to feed the world. We don't need to feed the world. We need to feed communities, create systems where communities grow for each other. Some grow tomatoes, some maize, some soy. They are self-sustaining.
>
> Scaling has caught on with other regions. Most are talking about exporting to other economies, other countries. We need to start with our own country. We need to grow and eat tomatoes rather than focusing on exporting to China because there's a bigger profit margin to export.

If you stay local, you are perfecting the market before you try to export. Those who are exporting have been in it for a while. They have made it. The margins are great, but standards are very high, and I can't meet that if I am a small farmer. We need to have patience.

Marc Nkaya Passongo Severin, a social entrepreneur from Republic of the Congo, offered, "Changing a portion of my country. I don't have to change the country. Change one village without gaining something from them. They will talk, giving motivation to others. That's how you bring change to a country—one village at a time."

Finally, Oscar Muriu, senior pastor of Nairobi Chapel, observed,

In the West, you're always asking to scale things up. You think one size fits all in any culture, but culture is so different! Trying to plant something that grows in sandy soil in muddy soil doesn't work. It takes time and investment. There's always the pressure to find something that works and then rubber-stamp it everywhere. I've seen it tried on me and it makes me run. I've become somewhat skeptical. Until you learn and engage the culture, you won't know what works. In Africa, we never say no. Part of that is our culture. We can't say no because it's a shame-based culture. We commit and say yes, but in our hearts, we're saying no.

This friction ties back to the foundational question—what is the primary problem that needs to be solved in many Majority World countries? The sixth area of friction deals with a foundational question as well—the primacy of individual rights vs. the common good.

6. THE VALUE OF INDIVIDUAL LIVES VS. THE VALUE OF COMMUNITIES

One of the more poignant exchanges I have seen around the question of the West's role in the Majority World occurred between Dambisa Moyo and Bill Gates after Moyo's book *Dead Aid: Why Aid is Not Working and How There Is a Better Way for Africa* was released. Moyo argued that international aid had led to many countries' dependence on outside bodies, encouraged government corruption, and kept economies from achieving sustainable economic growth. Her recommendation was to end aid, forcing African nations to make themselves more attractive to private investment.

When asked for his opinion of Moyo's book, Gates responded,

> It depends on your value system…. Having children not die is not creating a dependency, having children not be so sick they can't go to school, not having enough nutrition so their brains don't develop. That is not a dependency. That's an evil thing and books like that— they're promoting evil.[83]

Americans have a deeply held desire to save lives, to keep people from suffering. We are also individualistic people, and we tend to identify with individuals and their needs. Take for example the fact that more than $3 billion is donated by Americans each year for child sponsorship.[84] The emphasis with this approach is having a specific child that the sponsor financially supports throughout their childhood. They receive pictures of the child, develop a relationship through correspondence, and can even take a trip to meet the child in person. The relationship is focused on an individual child even though many sponsorship organizations openly support community development with a substantial portion of the sponsorship funds.

David Edson, an American social entrepreneur who grew up in India, commented about the role of individuals' photos in telling the story of need in the Majority World. "In America, we tend to focus on the depressing pictures. That's the way organizations make money— 'flies in the eyes pictures' that they get in a community. The reality is that could be one child in the community. That may not reflect the rest of the community at all." The pictures emphasize the worst situations, true, but do not miss the fact that they also personalize the problem. They reflect the American value of helping *individuals*, of making a difference in *one person's life*.

People in many Majority World countries, on the other hand, think in terms of "we" and what is good for the collective. Laud Basing offered the following as a way to make sense of the tension that exists specifically between Americans' desire to save lives and the desire of many in the Majority World to empower and restore entire communities, which can at times supersede the need to save a single life:

> We believe in society. We believe that a child is taken care of by the collective. We believe that individual life is superseded by the good of the people. A lot of people in the U.S. believe in individual rights. I have my rights no matter what society feels about it. That is a reason why we have a lot of conflict with people from the U.S. who are trying to do good. Each individual life is important, but what is good for the community is more important....
>
> In the U.S. it is more the individual. It is your conscience that makes you decide. If you do not have an issue in your conscience, you are good to go.

Jona Ambuga from Namibia also described the tension he feels as he works with NGOs and social enterprises from many countries:

They are failing because they never took the time to understand the *community*. I understand what you want us to do, but this is not what our *community* wants. If you are not willing to do what the *community* wants, thank you but no thank you.

Gerald Joseph from Haiti described this same commitment to the collective in some of the communities where Expedition Ayiti, an adventure-tourism social enterprise, brings hikers to stay overnight:

The money that goes to the [host] family, all of that money doesn't go to feed the hikers. Some is used to make small projects, to pay for schooling for small children in the community. Also, some communities use money for planting trees, paying for the school.

Tammy Grainger, an American who lived in Cote d'Ivoire for more than a decade, offered her perspective about this tension between individual and group rights, and specifically between the drive to save individual lives and the drive to grow as a society:

They view death differently and experience it differently. For us, most people couldn't imagine a child dying. I probably went to more funerals and saw more people die in my time there than most people would in a couple of lifetimes. That's the reality. So, it's hard for them to lose a child, but it's more the norm. It's not that they have a lesser view of the individual, it's just the reality, but they experience it differently. If you go to a funeral in the U.S., you will see people weep. In Cote d'Ivoire, they wail. They grieve for a week, but then they can move on. They do healthy grieving … do they ever grieve. The contrast is here you see tears, but Americans hold on to the grief. It goes with them for much longer.

Why is empowering communities so important to people in the Majority World?

As Basing explained, "Each individual life is important, but what is good for the community is more important."

People from the United States, the most individualistic culture in the world, and those from collectivist cultures do indeed approach the goal of progress from fundamentally different perspectives.

7. THE ROLE OF LAW AND THE NATURE OF ETHICS

A final area of friction mentioned in the interviews revolved around the role of law and ethics in a society. Most Americans who have spent time in the Majority World quickly realize that the role of rules and laws, and the definition of ethical behavior, can vary significantly across cultures.

According to Gary Hipp, a medical doctor who has spent more than four decades living in the Majority World, "Accountability for money is huge for Westerners. It's softer for the Majority World." Michael Grainger, an American who worked for an NGO in Cote d'Ivoire for more than a decade observed, "Here [in the United States] there are rules, law, and order. There, there are not."

This behavior can lead to high levels of frustration for Americans. One social entrepreneur working in East Africa described his experiences this way; "We have many conversations with Phoebe that turn more and more unpleasant. We feel that we are being gamed so we decide to pull the plug." And again, "We are getting concerned about Simon because our conversations with him are getting more contentious. He is not getting the data we need to us, not using the iPad, and making many excuses."

A Ghanaian social entrepreneur offered that Americans are indeed often gamed in his country:

If an American comes to Ghana, the best way is to look for someone in Ghana who understands the system. Work through the system. It's cheaper that way. Everyone believes everyone from the U.S. is rich. If you need to get something done in a rural community, what you are going to end up with is people trying to extort money from you. They are interested in helping themselves more than the community.

Daliso Chitundu, a social entrepreneur from Zambia, also observed, "People say yes to things but don't mean yes. Oh, I'll agree because I'll receive a paycheck, I'll get funding, but I don't think it will work. Americans are very straight forward."

This is certainly a very different approach to pricing and negotiations than Americans are used to. Jeanine Solo, a Burundian involved in community development, observed a common American response to this scenario: "I think Americans do not trust people. For example, there are some who cannot trust a business with Africans without an American on the team leading."

These seven points of friction are listed again below.

Common Points of Friction

1. The pace of work and enterprise expansion
2. The nature of business relationships
3. The primacy of innovation vs. restoration
4. The approach to introducing a new product
5. The value of scaling
6. The value of individual lives vs. the value of communities
7. The role of law and the nature of ethics

COMMENTARY

Clearly, the numerous differences explored in this chapter often lead to substantial friction. We'll consider several possible outcomes from this friction in the next chapter. But before I close this discussion, I want to explore the possibility that there is more going on under the surface than many Americans realize or acknowledge. What if some areas of friction not only reflect significant cultural differences but also an attempt to balance the power disequilibrium that often exists between Americans and those they are trying to help?

David Edson, who spent much of his childhood in India, has worked for social enterprises on several continents. He now directs a food-based social enterprise in the United States. He described experience with international development power dynamics in Haiti:

> We took on this orphanage project. It was a terrible orphanage. We brought teams in, worked with locals to build a new facility. We did lots of things to make it better for the kids and we really engaged them. We came back a year later and the roof of the main dorm was missing. When we asked the leaders, they told us, "We sold it. If we have no roof, people will see that we don't have one and will give us more money."
>
> It is the same with shoes. People give shoes to them and they sell them, so they will get more. The idea they have is, "As long as people are sympathetic toward us, we will be doing fine."
>
> What are they doing with the roof or shoe money? Americans have a hard time with this. It's been survival mode for these people forever. For them, they value having money to buy food rather than having a roof over their head. They will sell what you put in to buy what they actually need for their families to survive.

Americans may readily classify this type of response to outside help as corruption. And that it may be. But it is also useful to consider whether this friction is a response to relationships where one party holds most of the power and there seems to be no other way to alter the power balance. Roland Hoksbergen, an American economics professor who married a Guatemalan woman and lived for years in Latin America, described the unequal power dynamics this way. "Businesspeople want to come in with a business solution. They don't learn the language. Cultural intelligence gets ignored. They're like a bull in a china shop. They are powerful and get things done, but they are potentially disruptive."

Oscar Muriu, senior pastor of Nairobi Chapel, offered,

> One of the presumptions is that those who come from a money-centered economy have the power to dispense gifts and blessings to everyone else. That is a power question, and it is an arrogant question. If you give me 100 million shillings, I can get the job done. If you give me one million dollars. I dare say for most of us, we still believe that. Just give me the money.

Americans may be tempted to characterize the story of selling the orphanage's roof as just another example of corruption and the limitations of international aid, but the story offers us much more. Could it be that selling the roof was a means of empowerment because it allowed orphanage leaders to highlight their dignity and agency rather than their dependency? Basic human needs were met as leaders made a decision that reflected *their* highest priority—which did not happen to be a roof. Although Americans believed they had engaged the Haitian leaders in decision-making, true empowerment seemed to come through a decision that was made completely independent of the Americans. If the primary goal is empowerment—as many from the Majority World told me—is it possible that the decision the orphanage leaders made could be applauded by the Americans seeking to help them?

From the perspective of many Majority World leaders whom I interviewed, Americans enter a country moving fast, staying distant from the people they want to help, introducing outside "fixes" to very complex problems, and using a counter-cultural approach to sell their ideas. Americans may be able to "fix" some things with the power they hold, but they may not be the most important things to improve in the minds of local people. When different prices are charged to foreigners, donated roofs are sold for cash, or people say yes but mean no, this may reflect the most effective means Majority World people have to shift power between Americans and themselves.

PERSPECTIVES

Reflect on the points raised in the commentary then discuss your thoughts with someone from another culture.

Within every culture exist means for equalizing power. What do you believe are some of the most effective means for equalizing power in your culture? Why do you believe these approaches are especially effective?

Are there inherent benefits to restoration that innovation cannot offer? Discuss your ideas with someone who has a culturally different background than you.

Around which of the seven areas of friction described in this chapter have you personally experienced the most tension? Why?

Twelve

Power That Prevails

"True peace is not merely the absence of tension:
it is the presence of justice."

Martin Luther King, Jr.

Throughout the first eleven chapters, I have intentionally emphasized the role culture plays in explaining different approaches to development work. Recognizing cultural differences is essential for sense-making. But cultural differences alone do not usually lead people to say, "Go home" or "Leave us alone to address our problems."

The topic of power must also be included in this discussion because numerous Majority World and American leaders I interviewed believed it was an important topic to broach. Power is a dangerous thing when it allows us to isolate ourselves from the problem we hope to solve and when the power is great enough to push through a solution that is not valued or trusted by the intended beneficiaries.

The remainder of this book adds a power lens to the culture lens I have relied on thus far. Looking through this lens, there were three primary outcomes that I encountered in my research on American-led or co-led social enterprises in the Majority World.

1. The intended customers hold substantial power and use it to shut down or significantly limit the growth of an enterprise that is producing friction. This scenario was presented in Chapter 2.
2. Americans hold most of the power and use it to push past the friction, building an enterprise that may not reflect the values and goals of the people it is intended to serve. This scenario is explored in the remainder of this chapter.
3. Power is shared between Americans and nationals, who together work through friction to build an enterprise that has a greater positive impact than Americans or nationals could likely realize alone. Enterprises that fit this description are presented in Chapters 14 through 18.

THE GOOD LIFE

At the beginning of Chapter 10, Melinda French Gates' comment that we all want to give our children the same good things set the stage for a discussion about assumptions. She made another comment in the same interview that also gave me pause:

> I have had the huge privilege of spending time overnight, several nights in a row, with my oldest daughter, Jen, in a Massai home in Tanzania. We're out milking the cow under the stars. There's no light at night. We're trying to put a meal on the table and clean dishes. I know what life is like. And that could be me. That could be me and my daughter Jen or me and my son Rory living that life.

Do Americans indeed enjoy a better life because of our material wealth and advanced technologies as Melinda French Gate's comment seems to imply? According to many Majority World leaders with whom I spoke, Americans often enter a culture assuming they come from a place of strength and can help others arrive at that place as well. If we focus on an economic problem, this assessment of relative strength is logical. But throughout previous chapters, I have provided evidence that Americans and people from Majority World countries may not share a common definition of "the good life." Healthy relationships, balance between work and rest, the ability to care for others in your community— these are meaningful ways people evaluate their life beyond the accumulation of material goods. How accurate then is Americans' assumption that we have what others need simply because we are further along the path of economic development than they are?

I want to consider the characteristics of a flourishing society, but first we must decide who will define this. Sixty-three percent of Sub-Saharan Africans[85] and 88 percent of Latin Americans identify as Christian.[86] Worldwide, 55 percent of the world's population identifies as either Christian (31 percent) or Muslim (24 percent).[87]

As Stanford Chabaya, a Zimbabwean social entrepreneur explained, "Religion is especially prevalent here. They do go to church, they do worship. It's part and parcel of people's day-to-day lives, part of their daily routine. The Church tends to have lots of influence that can bring about change."

Religion plays a central role in many Majority World cultures and addresses questions related to meaning and purpose. It, therefore, seems appropriate to consider this question of societal flourishing using religious teaching as a starting point. The Jewish Torah, which is also the first five books of the Christian Old Testament, is considered by Jews, Christians, and Muslims to be sacred writing. The laws and societal institutions described in the Torah put forward a concrete means to measure a flourishing society.

FLOURISHING

The Torah's topics relating to society are broad, but they can be distilled into eight important teachings. Brief descriptions of each of these themes follow as they are developed in a publication titled *The Jubilee Roadmap*.[88] With regard to:

- Finance/The Economy – the emphasis should be on active rather than passive forms of income; debt ideally plays a very minimal role in society
- Property – should be owned by an extended family and kept in the family permanently
- Government – should be focused on local, community-based systems; any centralized government should serve a facilitating role to local entities
- Justice – should be a collaborative, restorative, community-based system
- Welfare – system should emphasize reintegration into a community and mutual obligation; family, work, and property play key roles in reintegration
- Community – should focus on long-term relationships across generations and different spheres of life
- Work/Rest – everyone should take one day of rest each week; time is used to invest in family and friends, rest, and recovery
- Family – ideally shared central identity, multigenerational, mutually supporting; the core of society

The following diagram, adapted from graphics developed by the Jubilee Center, highlights the integrated nature of society. Regardless of whether you believe the Torah is sacred writing, these themes offer an integrated vision of a flourishing society that can form the basis for identifying problems as well as solutions. The framework allows us to step back and recognize that the complexities facing every society demand a complex solution. Likewise, focusing on one area inevitably affects other aspects of society—for better or for worse.

An Integrated View of Society

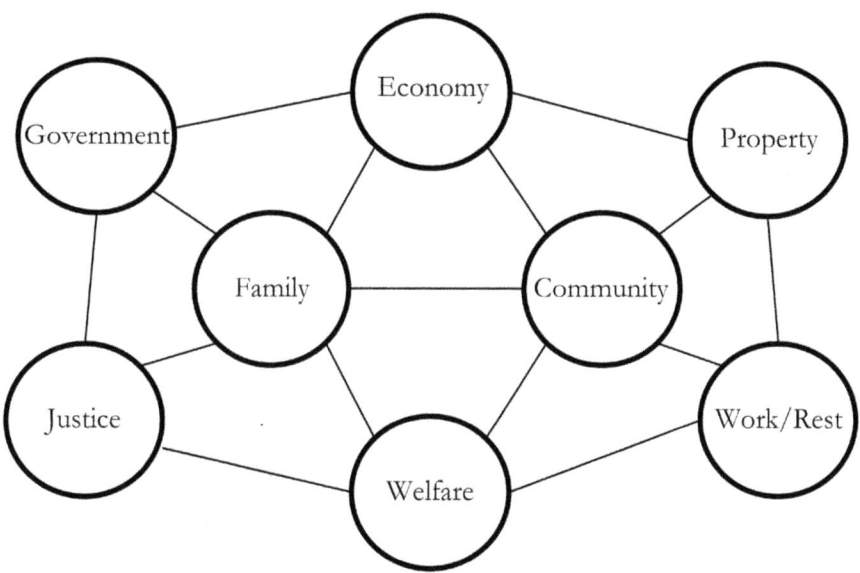

THE NATURE OF CHANGE

The Majority World social entrepreneurs in this study addressed the economic portion of the framework, but they also spoke of community, work/rest, family, and government as crucial aspects of societal flourishing during the interviews. For example, Global Bamboo Products Limited (Chapter 11) sought to maintain a balance between employees' work and rest, Haute Baso expressed interest in employees' family members (Chapter 8), and Life Medical Services (Chapter 3) emphasized community and welfare. Leaders of these enterprises seemed to perceive that their work was occurring within a system of many integrated parts. As they supported economic growth, they also strove to keep healthier aspects of society, such as work/life balance, intact. The American social entrepreneurs, on the other hand, more often focused on the economic portion of the framework. The following diagram portrays how society might look through a strong economic lens.

Society through an Economic Lens

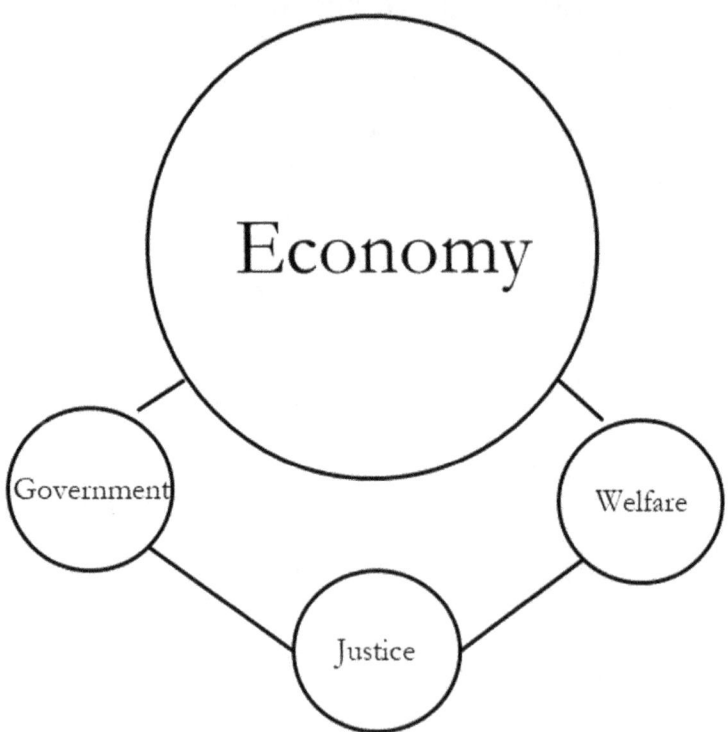

For every change that social entrepreneurs successfully introduce, there is a ripple effect that touches multiple parts of society. This ripple effect does not mean we should discourage economic development, but we must be very careful of the approach we take and its societal implications. Paul Nelson, retired CEO of the Crowell Trust, observed this after tracking the outcomes of funded projects for years:

> Change is foundational to this discussion. Donors and investors don't want things to stay the same. If there's a

presumed agreement that something needs to be changed, then you also need to explore the value of leaving things the way they are. What do you lose in the process of changing culture? If there isn't a strong sense of a need for change, there are some prior discussions that need to occur. Otherwise, it will come to the category of, "If you want to do that, go ahead. But it's gone once you're gone. We aren't buying into this."

If that's how things play out, there's anger afterward if we can't go back and do it the way we did it before. Cultural change is not neutral.

I certainly heard this sentiment repeatedly from Majority World leaders. Ghanaian Marigold Adu, for example, explained, "We sit with our arms folded and say, 'Go ahead and fail. What you consider wealth is different from what we consider wealth or a good life.'"

THE PRICE OF CHANGE

Change comes with a price. New technologies or new businesses are not introduced in isolation. They shape multiple aspects of a culture. According to Hofstede, the cultural scholar whom I have cited several times,

> Outside influences on a culture come from two main sources—forces of nature and forces of man. The latter includes trade, domination, and scientific discovery. The ultimate consequences of these forces include changes to the structure and functioning of institutions including family patterns, role differentiation, social stratification, socialization emphases, educational systems, religion, political systems, legislation, architecture, and theory development.[89]

Let's consider how new technologies shaped American culture in recent decades. Andy Crouch, author of *Culture Making: Recovering Our Creative Calling*, used the specific example of the highway system as a technology that was introduced with dramatic implications. Rivers were the traditional means of transportation. Cities had grown where two or more rivers intersected and technologies had been developed to make river transportation more efficient. The introduction of highways presented new opportunities including the growth of suburbs, new cities where highways intersected, and a trucking system to transport goods across the country.[90] However, with the new transportation system also came many people's departure from urban centers, the decline of some cities located a distance from the new highways, and a decline in the demand for some trades. The introduction of a new technology brought about numerous changes, including some that reshaped society in unanticipated ways.

Economic development more broadly has contributed to dramatic changes in American culture. Over the past century, Americans have increasingly focused on consumption and equating the good life with the acquisition of goods.[91] A former focus on thriftiness has shifted to commercialism and an expectation that we must have the latest model because the old one is obsolete.[92] This emphasis on consumerism is a defining characteristic of our culture today, whether it is the consumption of fine foods, the latest technology, or a new car.

A second major shift in American culture is increased individualism. According to Hofstede,

[W]e can assume that as long as the wealth of nations grows, the individualism of those nations' citizens will increase…. With increasing wealth, family patterns shift from the extended to the nuclear family.

The explanation of the causal relationship from wealth toward individualism is that poverty makes people depend on the support of their in-groups, but when a country's wealth increases, its citizens get access to resources that allow them to "do their own thing." The storyteller in the village market is replaced by television sets, first one per village, but soon more. In wealthy Western family homes, every family member may have his or her own TV set. The caravan through the desert is replaced by a number of buses, and these by a larger number of motor cars until each adult family member drives a different car. The village hut in which the entire family lives and sleeps together is replaced by a house with a number of private rooms. Collective life is replaced by individual life.[93]

As Americans have become more focused on consumption and more individualistic, changes have occurred in how we relate to others. For example, we are increasingly isolated, in part because we work so many hours and technology allows us to isolate ourselves. Over the past few decades, the average size of our social networks has declined by one-third and social networks have become less diverse.[94] Forty-nine percent of Americans report having three or fewer close friends,[95] and more than 58% of Americans reported being lonely in 2021.[96] Contributing to this loneliness and isolation is the fact that approximately 40 percent of first marriages and 70 percent of remarriages end in divorce, and 28 percent of American adults now live alone.[97]

In recent years, stress is also up, and rest is down. In 2018, 55 percent of American adults reported experiencing stress much of the previous day, compared to 35 percent globally. This was the highest stress level Americans had reported in a decade.[98] At any point in time, 7 percent of the U.S. adult population is dealing with major depression, and 19 percent is struggling with an anxiety disorder.[99, 100] Given all of these indicators, it is not completely surprising that, since 2014, the United States has been facing a declining life expectancy.

Major contributors were drug overdoses and suicides among young and middle-aged adults of all races.[101]

These changes are not all a direct result of economic development, but they have occurred as we have rapidly expanded our nation's wealth. They led James Doty, founder and director of the Center for Compassion and Altruism Research and Education at Stanford University to ask, "Why, in a country that consumes 25 percent of the world's resources, is there an epidemic of loneliness, depression, and anxiety? Why do so many in the West who have all of their basic needs met still feel impoverished?"[102]

When American society is considered as a complex system rather than strictly as an economic entity, it would be difficult to argue that it is flourishing. This conclusion could be drawn simply by looking at measures related to the family and work/rest portions of the Integrated View of Society diagram presented earlier in this chapter, but there is ample evidence that American welfare, justice, property, government, and community systems are not flourishing either.

- Welfare – People with mental illness are nine times more likely to be incarcerated than hospitalized.[103]
- Justice – Today the United States makes up about 5 percent of the world's population but has almost 25 percent of the world's prisoners; assuming current trends continue, one of every three black American males born today will go to prison in his lifetime.[104]
- Property – As of 2021, the top ten percent of households, as measured by net worth, owned 70 percent of the country's wealth. Since 2007, wealth has declined for all but the top 20%.[105]
- Government – A Gallup poll found that 3 percent of Americans have a great deal of confidence in our legislative branch; 62 percent have not very much or no confidence[106] and only 21 percent of Americans believe the government can be trusted to do what is right.[107]

- Community – A Gallup poll found 15 percent of blacks compared with 44 percent of whites are satisfied with the way blacks are treated in the U.S.[108]

Millions of voices are now crying out, demanding greater justice and equality in American society. Clearly, economic development is not the answer to all of these societal problems.

THE NEED FOR JUSTICE

The challenges facing Majority World countries are multifaceted as well and require more than an economic answer. Injustices, for example, must also be addressed if these societies are to flourish. Prabhu Guptara, Distinguished Professor of Global Business, Management, and Public Policy at William Carey University, India, described this crucial need for justice in the Majority World:

Many developing countries are ruled by thieves and murderers. A person can work within the envelope as a social entrepreneur, but the key issue is not that they need expertise or monetary support. The key issue is tyranny. Their culture predisposes them to tolerate tyranny. What's the end goal? Financial security or justice? Self-sufficiency or *shalom*?

Reports, such as the one produced by a 2008 United Nations commission, speak to the essential role of justice for societal well-being:

This Commission argues that four billion people around the world are robbed of the chance to better their lives and climb out of poverty because they are excluded from the rule of law. Whether living below or slightly above the poverty line, these men, women, and children lack the protections and rights afforded by the law. They may be citizens of the country in which they live, but their resources, modest at best, can neither be properly protected nor leveraged. Thus, it is not the absence of assets or lack of work that holds them back, but the fact that the assets and work are insecure, unprotected, and far less productive than they might be.[109]

Gary Haugen, President and Chief Executive of the International Justice Mission, expanded on this finding:

Throughout the developing world, public justice systems are being replaced with private systems of security and dispute resolution. The implications for the world's poorest people are devastating. Businesses and economic elites in developing countries left frustrated by incompetent police, clogged courts, and hopelessly overburdened judges and prosecutors are increasingly circumventing these systems and buying their own protection.... [I]n Guatemala, private security forces outnumber public police 7 to 1.

The repercussions extend far beyond the elites and businesses that buy safety. When protection must be purchased, the poorest are left with nothing to shield them from violence. In many developing countries, if you want to be safe, you pay to be safe. And if you can't pay to be safe—you aren't.[110]

Justice, welfare, economics, government … these facets of societies are deeply intertwined. If people are truly to flourish, then multiple, complex societal changes must take place. Simply changing a community's or region's economics is not enough.

When viewed with this complexity in mind, bringing about sustained improvement is an overwhelming task for any person. From this vantage point, no one needs to tell Americans, "Go home," because they may choose to do so on their own. But this is where the value of combining assets becomes central to the discussion. No one engineer, no one businessperson, no one economist can bring about substantial change by themselves. These pressing, complex needs demand the assets of many people who see themselves as important contributors to a story that is far bigger than themselves.

It can be easy for Americans to consider our level of economic development and assume that we must share our knowledge and skills with others. We may even be tempted to use our power to push through an idea we believe will bring about positive change. But if this change occurs as nationals "Sit with our arms folded and say, 'Go ahead and fail. What you consider wealth is different from what we consider wealth or a good life,'" it is the wrong kind of change.

So how does one pivot to a better path? At an individual level, progress starts by identifying our assumptions. This can be a very powerful exercise for people from any culture. Andy Crouch, in *Culture Making: Recovering Our Creative Calling*, offered five questions to ask, which are adapted below.

1. What do we assume about the way the world is?
2. What do we assume about the way the world should be?
3. What does my product or service make possible?
4. What does my product or service make impossible or very difficult?
5. What new forms of culture are created in response to my product or service?[111]

As you ask these questions, two things hopefully occur. First, you recognize the responsibility you are taking upon yourself in defining how the world is and should be (Questions 1 and 2). Second, you realize you are unable to answer fully Questions 3 through 5 due to limited knowledge about the implications of the change you are trying to introduce. Your self-sufficiency comes into question, which is a healthy response to have.

If we define the problem of flourishing in terms that encompass just two of the eight societal components described earlier in this chapter, the solution quickly becomes more than any one person or homogeneous team can easily address. Humility becomes essential at this point—the humility, particularly for Americans, to acknowledge the potential damage unbridled power can inflict. And for American and Majority World leaders alike, the humility to recognize that others' distinct skills, experiences, and connections can be invaluable if their work is to bring about true flourishing.

During the interviews, people identified a number of different assets that American and Majority World entrepreneurs often bring to their work, assets that complement each other and, when combined, allow for greater positive impact. The next chapter explores these different assets and Chapters 14 through 18 describe social enterprises that directly benefited from collaboration.

PERSPECTIVES

American social values are some of the most advanced in the world. It is Americans' responsibility to encourage other societies to adopt these values.

It is a leader's responsibility to be aware of how their product or service could result in unintended negative consequences for the people they are trying to help.

Under what conditions are these statements true? Under what conditions are they false?

Section 3

Partnership

This final section takes a very practical look at how five sets of American and Majority World leaders have combined their strengths to build enterprises that neither party could have built alone. Commonalities among the five enterprises are highlighted as well as concrete ways leaders operationalized goals of empowerment and collaboration. Barriers to this collaborative approach are explored followed by an honest look at the opportunities for flourishing that lie before us all.

The driving questions in this section are:

- What complementary strengths can Americans and nationals often contribute to a social enterprise?
- What are examples of combined assets being harnessed for the common good in the Majority World?

Thirteen

Distinct Assets

*"It is very hard to learn from someone
if you think they have nothing to teach you."*

Michael Ramsden

I ended the last chapter considering the complexity involved in societal flourishing and the need for multiple players' assets to bring about sustainable improvement. During my interviews with Majority World leaders, many named assets they value in Americans, assets they need, and cannot easily acquire within their normal networks. These Majority World leaders also named crucial assets for building enterprises that they possess, assets that Americans do not or could not typically possess. This chapter names and describes these two sets of assets and offers examples of them in action.

AMERICANS' MOST VALUABLE ASSETS

Majority World leaders whom I interviewed noted four valuable assets Americans can contribute as an enterprise is being built: entrepreneurial vision and expertise, technological skills, social access, and the ability to secure financial capital. We'll explore each of these in turn below.

1. Entrepreneurial Vision and Expertise

Unlike people in many Majority World countries, Americans have a long and successful history of launching businesses. Klein Ileliji co-leads JUA Technologies International, a social enterprise built around a solar dryer he designed. His Nigerian heritage, years spent living in the United States, and extensive work around the world as an agricultural and biological engineering consultant provide a unique vantage point from which to speak:

> The culture of having kids sell lemonade—you might think it's small but it's there, that model. In my children's [American] school, they had a lemonade contest. The children brought recipes, had stands, competed for who made the most amount of money. The children learned selling.
>
> In a lot of these [Majority World] countries, training for enterprise doesn't happen in schools or in the universities. The system does not support business start-ups.
>
> Having your mother sell on the street is demeaning. There's nothing dignified about entrepreneurship. I studied agricultural engineering. My dad said, "What is that? That's like working with the poor farmers." When a child hears farming, they see a poor guy in tattered clothes who cannot feed himself or have a home. The farmers in most parts of Africa are farming because they

have no option. The guy with a car dealership—that guy is making money. He has a choice. The sellers on the streets, hawking, they are surviving. They have nothing else.

Wilfrid Marx Abidji, from Benin, also spoke to the need for entrepreneurial training—something around which he has helped build a social enterprise:

> For decades we've been taught that working for the government is better. The government is the single job supplier. But we realize that the government now is unable to employ all college graduates, so people are finally starting their own businesses. They will starve if they wait for the government to hire them.
>
> Being an entrepreneur is a question of passion in the U.S. In Benin, it's a question of constraint. Entrepreneurial training should show how to be an entrepreneur from your heart, not because of constraints. The difference is that there are many opportunities in the U.S.
>
> We learn entrepreneurship nowhere. There is no school for it in Benin. Our political history includes communism where every business is state-owned. This did not prepare our minds for entrepreneurship, so we have a need for training to change people's minds.

2. Technological Skills

Abidji also described many technological skills Americans could offer an enterprise in a Majority World country:

> Companies like mine need skilled engineers. We need a sealer to seal this bag one of my companies is making. We need a cassava dryer to be made with local parts.
>
> Importation is the norm. People are not used to buying Benin products, so market development—how

to help people start buying locally. Economically, how to add value to an agricultural product, how to have access to a market. Then there will be permanent movement up the value chain.

Outside partners should be catalytic. They should add value to the product. Money is secondary. It is not the problem.

3. Social Access

Beyond technological skills, access to markets through one's networks was mentioned as an asset Americans can offer. Joachim Ewechu, co-founder and CEO of SHONA, observed an additional value that can result from Americans' involvement with an enterprise—preferential treatment because of one's standing in a society:

> Sometimes having an expat[riate] gives us more weight. Our program brings together for five weeks investors and entrepreneurs in a big house. We had a local person looking for a facility. He was sent to find something and book it for next year, but he was blown off the next day. He had found a relatively new property that was very big, and they were building their business. When the local team member asked about renting it, he was told it was not available for rent.
>
> "Ivan, this is crazy," I said. "We have a big network that we would tell about this place. We want to book it for fifty people for five weeks. We could give them so much business." So, I had Kate go with him the next day. She brought credibility and confidence because Ivan brought the "white guy." They let her sign an agreement that day to rent the place. It made all the difference to have her there.

I asked, "You and Ivan are young. Did Kate's presence add credibility because she's older as well as American?"

Ewechu replied, "She is twenty-six and female. It's strictly about being an expat, not about being older or male."

Doug Taylor, who co-leads Expedition Ayiti, an adventure-tourism social enterprise in Haiti, also described this dynamic:

> Because I have white skin, I can have conversations and get meetings that they [my Haitian partners] could never get. Ideally, they oversee everything in Haiti, all the logistics, meetings with others who want to work with us. But when we went into a meeting with the Ministry of Tourism, talking about developing other eco-tourism routes in other parts of Haiti, they were always looking at me. The conversation was with me.

4. Ability to Access Financial Capital

A fourth asset several Majority World leaders described is Americans' experience with accessing financial capital. A Sri Lankan NGO leader observed, "Americans understand how to write proposals, how to evaluate projects."

Daliso Chitundu, a Zambian social entrepreneur, commented,

> Help Africans write proposals. We don't know how to access financing. Training is what we need, not more money. When you are a baby, you have to be fed. As you grow up, you want to learn to cook, to feed yourself.
>
> I was at an awards ceremony—agricultural awards. Millions were being awarded. Seven of the eight awards went to white people. I was sitting at a table with a Kenyan and an Ethiopian. We just looked at each other. We don't know how to access money that's designed for us. We don't have access, but we have ideas.

MAJORITY WORLD LEADERS' MOST VALUABLE ASSETS

Numerous examples of Majority World leaders' unique assets for building an enterprise also wove through the interviews I conducted. These included a deep understanding of what it means to live in poverty, social capital, extensive knowledge of local resources, long-term commitment, patience, and understanding of how to empower people. Each of these assets is explored below.

1. Deep Understanding of Poverty

First, many Majority World leaders, particularly if they have lived in poverty themselves, comprehend the multiple facets of poverty in a way that outsiders cannot. "I've worked among the poor all my life. We know that the best workers among the poor are those who come from a poor background," observed a Sri Lankan leader.

2. Social Capital

Majority World leaders possess crucial social capital in their community and beyond. They have access to local opinion leaders as well as a level of trust with them because of their insider status. Cultural insiders also have intimate knowledge of how to function in their high-context society. Joachim Ewechu, co-founder and CEO of SHONA, observed,

> When you show up at a place, accept the fact that you are in a very different context. Accept that you have no idea what is happening. Be willing to learn.
> Local people have social pull in their community that outsiders do not have. This is especially important in collectivist cultures where in-groups are very powerful. When you are dealing with local small businesses, you need locals. Locals understand markets, the local context.

Some negotiations need a local person to deal with them. An expat can't. An expat is seen differently for pricing—everything goes up, so locals do the deal instead.

The beauty is a blended team. Expats get humbled by locals, and locals get challenged by expats. Expats are ahead of the game on some levels, thinking in some certain ways. Locals are saying, "Here things are done like this." An equal voice balance on the team is needed.

3. Extensive Knowledge of Local Resources

Stacey Eyman, an American who worked with an NGO in a rural part of Costa Rica, observed the valuable knowledge local people held:

> They didn't understand what they had to offer me, what they could teach me. They held the cards. I wish they had known that they have power to influence NGOs and white people. They know the area, they know about the culture, what the NGO needs to know. They know what's expected, how to survive. I wish they had seen the value of their own knowledge.

Fekadu Melese has tapped this asset personally in recent years. Born in Ethiopia, he earned a degree in civil engineering from Addis Ababa University and then worked there for more than twenty years as an engineer. He later moved to the United States to pursue a doctoral degree in engineering as well as his vision for addressing the housing challenges he observed in Ethiopia. In his words,

> Housing is a serious problem for many. My research has developed compression cement blocks. Compressed earth is the key. The dirt is tested for suitability and you can improve it by adding less than 10 percent cement

or lime to stabilize it. These blocks are strong, durable, insulated, and inexpensive. For thousands of years, our ancestors lived in the earth because it is insulated so well.

I have three business models to address low-income people. For the lowest of the low, I will rent the equipment to them, and they will make the houses personally using their own labor. They use septic systems, so they can dig a hole, and then that's the dirt you need for the house blocks. You help them with technical things. The machine uses levers and a fulcrum to make blocks. They can build their own house with this—a neat, beautiful home they can be proud of.

Perhaps an American could have come up with this idea. However, I suspect we would be more likely to create a solution using cutting-edge technology rather than work to stabilize Ethiopian dirt inexpensively.

4. Long-Term Commitment

Local leaders also bring a long-term, often life-long commitment to their work, which allows them to build a sustainable enterprise that is not dependent on outsiders.

Daliso Chitundu, a Zambian social entrepreneur, offered, "It's a personal thing. I will be here for sixty years. I want my child, my child's child, my child's child's child to enjoy this facility I'm building."

Joachim Ewechu, the Ugandan leader, commented, "When a crisis happens, expats pack up and leave. Then the company will fail. Continuity. We need continuity and locals bring that."

During an Ebola crisis, Global Mamas, a Ghanaian social enterprise, experienced this firsthand. According to Alice Grau,

We are trying to partner [locally] more because of the dramatic decrease of volunteers who really influenced our training programs. They went from seventy to fifteen due to the Ebola crisis. We are learning that we do not want to rely on international volunteers for training resources and instead we want to rely more on local resources and local volunteers.

5. Patience

Fifth, nationals often bring a slower pace, which in the long run, may prove to be invaluable. Students of cultural change observe a direct correlation between the rate of change and the longevity of the change—the slower the change occurs, the longer its impact is likely to be.[112]

Edwards, leader of the social enterprise Healthy Living (Chapter 2), observed this value in action. "Things move slower when a [national] leads it. That's not a bad thing."

6. Understanding of How to Empower Vulnerable People

Finally, many of the Majority World entrepreneurs recognized, within their cultural context, how to strengthen hope and dignity in those they were trying to support. Marigold Adu allowing employees to make their own decisions about when to work is one example (Chapter 11). Mavis Thandizo Kanjadza's patience in watching only two of ten women continue with her program is another (Chapter 4). Kanjadza knew the two women who remained would encourage others to join the program. She also knew she was empowering all ten of the women as they determined how they would build their own futures.

The following table highlights Majority World and American assets and visually displays ways in which they complement each other. Americans' assets largely reflect their leadership in global markets, in entrepreneurialism, and in innovation. I have added efficient use of time and optimism to the table, which are described in Chapters 5 and 7. Americans generally view these as assets, and a few from Majority World countries specifically mentioned valuing Americans' efficient use of time.

Majority World leaders' skills mentioned in the interviews largely reflect their unique strengths in the local culture—knowledge of local resources and cultural norms, social capital, and in many cases, intimate knowledge of poverty and its ability to strip people's hope and dignity. Patience and a slower pace appear in the table because, as indicated above, these too can play important roles in an enterprise's success.

The list of Majority World leaders' common strengths focuses on *unique* assets they can offer a multinational team, assets that Americans do not typically have. Many Majority World social entrepreneurs also have, for example, strong technological skills and significant social capital beyond a local community, but this table emphasizes assets that may be more commonly found in members of one culture or the other.

One set of skills is not more valuable than the other. If we use the analogy of a puzzle, the table depicts multiple pieces that come together to form a whole—a whole that is complete when *all* the parts are represented.

During my research, I came across five social enterprises that pooled assets in powerful ways: Aqua Clara International, Expedition Ayiti, IMON International, Global Mamas, and Floral. From the start, the enterprise leaders worked from the assumption that both sets of assets were essential for sustainability and positive impact.

In the next five chapters, each enterprise is described with commentary afterward. At the end of the five cases, I explore three distinct assumptions under which these enterprises operate. Together their stories provide a fascinating look at the benefits of pooling assets and sharing power in ways that bring about a greater good than either Americans or nationals could accomplish alone.

Complementary Assets	
American Assets	**Majority World Assets**
• Highly efficient use of time	• Patience, slower pace
• Exceptional optimism	• Long-term commitment
• Social access both inside and outside the country	• Social capital within the culture
• Technological skills and expertise	• Extensive knowledge of local resources
• Ability to access financial capital	• Understanding of what it means to live in poverty
• Entrepreneurial expertise	• Tacit knowledge of the local culture and constraints that exist within it
• Access to powerful global markets	• Understanding of how to empower vulnerable people

PERSPECTIVES

To what extent do you believe complementary assets are necessary for building a sustainable enterprise?

Americans launching an initiative in another culture must include people with an understanding of local culture and resources on their senior leadership team.

Under what circumstances do you believe this statement is true? Under what circumstances do you believe this statement is false?

What do you believe are your greatest assets for development work?

Fourteen

Aqua Clara International

"We only go where we are invited.
We don't have a marketing department."

Harry Knopke

This story begins in Traverse City, Michigan. Bob McDonald retired from Dow Chemical Midland in 2005, having worked in both business and marketing development around the globe.

"In my travels," he said, "I quickly learned that water is not always your 'friend.' It is capable of making you sick or even killing you. I saw that the poorest people often had no choice but to consume dirty water."

McDonald wanted to make a difference in his retirement, so he established Aqua Clara International (ACI) to provide "clean, cheap water" to people around the world.

THE CONTEXT

McDonald defined "clean, cheap water" as locally generated water that meets World Health Organization standards as inexpensively as possible. For it to be "cheap," the water purification process had to be inexpensive and use local materials. For it to be "clean," he engaged engineers and scientists at two universities to further develop biosand water purification. The result was a biosand filter that costs $12 USD or less to construct, less than $1 per year to operate, and lasts between five and ten years with minor maintenance.

Aqua Clara International now has three patented technologies with water purifiers in more than thirty-five countries that serve more than 330,000 people. These purifiers can generate up to 3,100,000 liters of clean water per day. The typical in-country cost for transforming one liter of contaminated water into one liter of clean water is $0.001 to $0.002 per liter. In 2010, ACI conducted a monitoring survey of biosand users in Kenya. They found that household income was less than $1 per person per day which confirmed for them that they are indeed reaching the poorest people with cheap, clean water.

THE MODEL

ACI uses a partnership-based entrepreneurial model. The businesses are based in rural schools, which are open to the community and provide a safe place for the materials to be stored as well as a demonstration site for the products. A school representative and the students who choose to join the Water and Hygiene Club care for and maintain all the ACI products that provide clean water for the school.

Community Development Entrepreneurs (CDEs) and Community Health Promoters (CHPs) play key roles in the businesses. The CDE, who is often identified by school leaders, operates a small ACI business. He or she has responsibility for social marketing as well as constructing and selling biosand filters, two types of safe-water-storage containers, and hand-washing containers to end-users. This person is also responsible for helping end-users learn how to use the filter, how to store treated water safely, and how to identify when filter maintenance needs to take place. The first time this maintenance occurs, the CDE returns to the buyer's home to provide hands-on assistance in properly completing this task.

I asked Harry Knopke, President of ACI and past university president, what qualifications the entrepreneurs (CDEs) normally have:

> It differs by setting. In Kenya, sixty have been trained. They are mostly farmers, but some have different skills. When this started, we didn't select any CDEs. They were selected by their villages. We only go where we are invited. We don't have a marketing department. We got invited in by some people in our area who had been working in Kenya for years and knew the need. They put ACI in touch with school officials who are the social hub of a community. So, once the schools asked for help, then the village elders around those schools selected who they knew to be honorable, trustworthy. As people got interested in this, it became a referral process. People in business didn't want their business ruined, so CDEs only referred good people to be CDEs.

The Community Health Promoters (CHPs) also play key roles in this business model. They are women from the local community who are hired to help promote good water hygiene and sanitation practices alongside the products being sold. They visit homes thirty to sixty days after the owner has purchased a biosand filter to check on construction standards and to be sure the user understands how to use the filter and how to store the water safely. This visit also includes simple training on hygiene and sanitation improvements. They return to the home twelve months after installation and again twenty-four months after installation to monitor the use of the biosand filters. The CHPs also provide safe water training to the students in the Water and Hygiene Clubs.

According to Chip Blatchlee, an engineering professor who has contributed to the project, "These are women—100 percent women. Water responsibilities fall on women in these communities. Women build greater trust with other women and are more eager to learn." ACI has also found that women are able to collect more honest responses during their site visits compared to men.

Once ACI has established a relationship with a school and a CDE and CHP have been chosen, the school launches a kick-off for the local business that includes local chiefs, neighbors, clubs, parents, and students. During the launch, a local ACI staff member explains how the program works, how to use the biosand filter, and introduces the CDE and CHP. Those in attendance then prepare sand and gravel for a demonstration filter installation. In addition to engaging attendees' participation and helping them understand the filter's importance, the launch acts as a public endorsement of the CDE and ACI.

According to Knopke,

We were invited to the Cite Soleil in Haiti by a couple of people. We heard from the Haitians, "You won't do anything. It's not worth our while to spend our time or our money with you, ACI." But we started with a couple of people who were serious about bringing clean water to the schools. Word got out that these people follow through on what they say, that there was an ongoing relationship with the schools, that kids were healthy. We didn't have to do any marketing. We did everything we could to keep up with the requests for filters because there was a great demand. We had demonstrated basic values and people began to trust us.

We don't go anywhere unless we are invited. That invitation needs to come from community members, NGOs, or other entities that have credibility and acceptable boots on the ground that we can collaborate with.

"What are the unique contributions that nationals make in ACI's business model?" I asked.

At even a very simplistic level, just getting from one place to another is important. Knowing who can get something done is very important. We've seen thousands of filters and wells that aren't used because people weren't taught to use and maintain them. There wasn't follow up. If nationals are vested in multiple levels in these programs, then sustainability is an achievable goal.

"Have you teamed with other community organizations besides schools?"

Yes, we have. But the reason for partnering with schools is practical as much as anything. In many of these countries, if a person has made it to adulthood, even if they get sick, it is likely they will live for many more years. But with kids, given childhood illnesses, that's not the case for them. They may die shortly.

There's another reason for working through the schools. Once children understand the value of clean water, they will tell their parents and get them to change their habits too. That's another great reason to focus on the young—they are marketers for us. Also, schools are politically neutral for the most part.

"What is a key strength of ACI?"

We have a system in place that lends itself to replication. Not cookie-cutter replication, though. We have fifteen schools in Nicaragua that have our large water filtration systems. Each is different. Not one is alike. The technology is flexible enough to fit into different circumstances.

"How did you come to do so many things apparently right?"

Bob McDonald [the founder of ACI] reached out to many people, many of whom didn't know him. Bob went all over … As we say on our website, our work is science-based. Not just basic physical science, but also social and behavioral sciences. Understanding that area and having my background has been valuable. I'm a behaviorist myself. Learning. Evolution. That's what's made us successful. It takes a lot of groundwork and a lot of patience. You can't push things. It takes time.

Hilda Romero Zepeda, a faculty member of the *Universidad Autónoma de Querétaro* in Mexico, has been working with Aqua Clara International for several years. I interviewed her about the experience of working with Aqua Clara International. She first described the problem that led to their collaboration:

Water contamination is the main reason children die below five years of age. It is not only organic contamination but also arsenic, mercury, metals, and metalloids. Mexico is in first place internationally in Coca-Cola consumption, so we are having obesity and diabetes issues now. That problem is increasing because we don't have secure sources of water.

We have been working with Aqua Clara to bring opportunities for indigenous communities to address their contaminated water. We also support public institutions in marginalized communities by working with indigenous schools. For example, we have put filters in five different schools.

"Tell me more about your work with villages in the state of Querétaro."

Water is the way we get into the community. In the end, they love us. Everything is because of water. Before Aqua Clara, I used to enter communities through nutrition, food. They thought we were insulting them because we were asking them what they ate. They were insulted because they could only afford to eat corn and beans. Water allows a different way in, one that does not insult them.

Once you get there, you realize there is another kind of problem that you can collaborate on. I had the opportunity to bring students from our Master of Psychology program, and they were able to work with family violence.

"What has it been like to work with Aqua Clara International leaders?"

It's a real doctor to doctor relationship, working together with them to help communities. They are humans trying to work with humans. There is no discrimination in working with us. The temperature is very high here. Theirs is very low [in Michigan]. They need to contrast everything. Harry [Knopke] was putting his hands in everything and trying to fix everything. They [Aqua Clara International leaders] are down on the ground. They are fixing things, and they are trying to do their best, registering data, and asking us to be serious with the data we are using. I really love them.

COMMENTARY

Aqua Clara International utilizes both national and American assets as they sell inexpensive water filters around the world. Local people oversee marketing, sales, and all follow-up training in the use of the filters. They use their social capital to engage communities with the filters, recognizing what will work in their context. They demonstrate the product and allow people to decide over time if they will buy the filter. Their long-term commitment is evident through follow up that occurs months and even years after a filter is purchased.

American technical, social, and financial assets are tapped as well. The filters and the business model were developed through experimentation by engineering, business, and social science professionals. Aqua Clara International began through the founder's personal connections in Kenya, and it has continued to grow through contacts made around the world. ACI has also successfully accessed the necessary financial capital to build this global organization.

Aqua Clara International tapped both American and national assets in powerful ways. But their approach was more distinctive than that. The American leaders also operated under assumptions that often run somewhat counter to American norms.

1. ACI leaders focused on empowerment, in part by assuming they would collaborate with local people from the start.

Their decision to wait for potential users to contact them rather than marketing their product is unusual, to say the least, but they assumed local people should decide for themselves whether they needed clean water. They, therefore, allowed local leaders to approach ACI through shared contacts rather than vice versa. This encouraged customers to buy into and take responsibility for their own clean water from the very beginning.

Romero also emphasized empowerment throughout our interview: "We have been working with Aqua Clara to bring opportunities for indigenous communities to address their contaminated water." Later she observed, "Once you get there, you realize there is another problem you can collaborate on."

Her comments indicate she too assumes the work must be collaborative with people in the villages if it is to bring about helpful change.

2. The ACI leadership team believed in local leaders' inherent resourcefulness and ability.

They operated with the assumption that local people had the ability to build and maintain their own filters, conveying respect and hope in the process. ACI personnel had come to a clear understanding of their personal strengths, including technical knowledge, financial resources, and safe water training materials. They also believed local people held essential assets that must be part of the mix including the ability to communicate in a culturally appropriate way with their customers and an understanding of barriers to filter buy-in from community members. Their belief in the strengths of the local people is a wonderful example of American optimism operating in a highly effective way.

As stated previously, Romero also described her own relationship with Aqua Clara International members as one characterized by humility and respect. "It's a real doctor to doctor relationship, working together with them to help communities. They are humans trying to work with humans. There is no discrimination in working with us."

3. ACI leaders understood the importance of building respect- and trust-based relationships as they introduced the filters into each community.

They utilized a community's existing trust in schools and local leaders to launch their product. Rather than choosing employees themselves, ACI leaders asked local people to select and refer entrepreneurs and health promoters. They also incorporated customer follow up and training into their business plan. Some of these steps took significant time but building trust and solid customer support were primary goals for ACI.

4. ACI leaders recognized the power of tradition and every person's hesitancy to change habits quickly.

For this reason, they engaged trusted community leaders who encouraged filter purchases. They also partnered with students whom they believed were more likely to adopt new behaviors and who could influence family members to do so as well. Finally, they invested in formal training in the schools so that students had firsthand knowledge and understanding of the importance of safe water and hygiene practices.

5. ACI leaders assumed they needed a variety of skills from different sectors.

ACI tapped into scientific expertise early on as they developed water filters, but they also sought out clean water materials from the World Health Organization to use as training materials for effective hygiene. As Knopke noted, they relied on his strengths as a social scientist when they put together their business model. They also continue to rely on their personal and professional connections around the world to introduce local people to their clean water products. This approach that assumes the need for a wide variety of skills and assets helps to explain their success in bringing clean water to more than a quarter-million people.

In summary, ACI leaders assumed:

- *Empowering local people is foundational to a social enterprise's mission.*
- *The resourcefulness and capability of the local people are key ingredients of a successful enterprise.*
- *The primacy of healthy relationships and the trust that flows from them are more important than achieving hard goals in a specific time frame.*
- *The powerful role of tradition and common resistance to new products must be addressed.*
- *Professional expertise from several sectors must be accessed. Business or technical skills alone could not provide all the skills and perspectives ACI would need to succeed.*

PERSPECTIVES

What did you notice in this case?

How does Aqua Clara International's approach differ from other social enterprises' approaches with which you are familiar?

Fifteen

Expedition Ayiti

"Expedition is not in our culture.
We don't really know what it means, 'hiking' ...
I didn't know it before because in Haiti
people walk for a reason."

Junior Auguistin

A second social enterprise that taps both local and American assets is anchored in the Caribbean. After graduating from college in the late 1970s, Doug Taylor lived for two years in Haiti, learning Creole in the process. Since then, he has traveled back to Haiti numerous times. In Taylor's words,

I made a visit to Haiti in 2009 and took Mike. He and his twin brother have been backpacking enthusiasts since Cub Scouts. As he and I were driving up into the Central Plateau Mike said, "Doug, this country would be a backpacker's dream. It's beautiful and there are all these natural walking trails. You can use those trails, and no one would have to maintain them. And the people are naturally hospitable." People fall in love with Haiti because of the hospitality of the people.

A couple of hours later we arrived in the little village of Pignon. That's where I lived for a few years when I was younger. We went to a tree where my friends always met in this little town. I spoke in Creole. "Hey, you guys. Mike's a backpacker and he says we should start a backpacking business."

They first asked, "What is backpacking?" They started laughing. "Who would ever pay to walk?" The main form of transportation is walking there. We said, "In the U.S. and Europe, people pay to go on hikes."

When you're in Haiti you're always thinking of enterprises that could make money. We talked about it at length. A few months later I was visiting Haiti again, January 2010, when the earthquake happened. I ended up being hired by Habitat of Haiti, so I was down there for two years after the earthquake. Habitat placed me close to Pignon, fifteen miles or so away. On the weekends, I'd go over and talk with them about this hiking business.

The fact that I was there for two years gave me a lot of time to be with them. We actually formed a route. They warmed up to the idea and agreed to it. We went to the communities where we'd be doing the overnight stays.

These rural communities aren't really towns. They're a bunch of people living in close proximity. There's usually a church and a school. We met with the leaders of all those communities where we wanted to stay overnight. We had several meetings with them, told them about the concept. Before I came home for good, we had our first hike and we've been hiking ever since.

PARTNERSHIP

Haitians Gerald Joseph and Junior Auguistin, along with Doug Taylor and his son Austin, decided to launch Expedition Ayiti, an adventure-tourism company. (Ayiti is the Creole name for Haiti, which means "land of mountains.") Participants are in Haiti for nine days, most of which is spent hiking through the mountainous central region. Along their journey, they sleep in Haitian homes in rural villages, eat local food, and share time with the families who are hosting them. Groups are led by Auguistin and others who describe the region's history and customs along the way.

Austin Taylor described Joseph and Auguistin's roles:

Gerald grew up in Haiti and went to school there. He's very smart and educated. He's the chief of the community. He doesn't hike. He's responsible for orientation, explaining Expedition Ayiti, and putting together the itinerary for the week. Junior is in charge of leading the hikes. He and I have a great time together.

In Joseph's words,

The guides in Haiti offer to our customers the body of Haiti. There is so much bad news about the country, but we want to make sure to show them that the country is not as bad as they show in the news. We want to show them our culture. We have some beautiful historical pages. The American can learn that even though you don't have much money and don't have a lot of commodities, you can live, and you can be happy without big money. First, they stay in the capital, but we also show them the different parts of Haiti and the history of our communities.

Joseph also explained that his mother played a role when the business was launching:

My mother had to teach the overnight leaders the way to cook and serve our hikers. That was her role, to teach hospitality, because in Haiti it's one of our most valued qualities. She not only taught them how to cook but what to cook for Americans and Europeans and how to treat them when they are there in our homes.

Doug Taylor added,

Rosalyn had worked for the Catholic Church in Pignon and cooked for the missionaries thirty-five years ago. She later worked in the hospital and cooked for them there, so she had thirty-five years of experience cooking for Americans.

Eighty percent of the hikers' fees are directed to hosts and in some cases to their communities. As Joseph explained it,

The money that goes to the family, that money doesn't all go to feed the hikers. Some is used to do small projects, to pay for schooling for small children in the community. Also, some communities use money to plant trees or pay for the school.

CHALLENGES

Running the business is not without its complexities. According to Doug Taylor,

One of the barriers is that a lot of people are really interested in doing this but when it comes down to it, they feel guilty for being a tourist in this poor country. "I don't want to go unless I can help," [they say].

Auguistin and Austin Taylor also spoke about challenges cultural differences can create. In Austin Taylor's words,

It's not always easy. There are cultural differences in how money and time are viewed. You give suggestions on how we need to treat people and to be timely, but it's not something that comes naturally because of the way they view things differently.

Working cross-culturally is really hard, even with the best intentions on both sides. Historically there's lots of baggage between the two groups of people. Even if you have good personal relationships, it's tough being on the same level and working toward the same goal. It's rewarding at the same time. Maybe that's the most important thing to come out of that—trying to understand each other.... They call my dad the Blond Haitian. They love him. Gerald named his son after him.

Auguistin also felt the tension of these cultural differences.

Expedition is not in our culture. We don't really know what hiking means, so it's the kind of thing I had to adapt to. I didn't know hiking before because in Haiti people walk for a reason. They leave a city to go to another city to do something. We walk far away, that we do, but for a reason. Expedition Ayiti is not for a reason. It's just for fun.

It was difficult to understand when they came to us with this idea. I said, "Okay, I'm going to see." But then people were thinking we are crazy because when they asked me, "Junior, where are you going?" and I said, "I am just hiking," they said, "What does it mean, 'hiking?'" I said, "I am just hiking."

COMMENTARY

As with the previous case, multiple players' assets are employed in this enterprise. Auguistin knows the trails, and Joseph is trusted by the families they invite to host hikers. Both men know their country's history and culture, which they share with hikers. Joseph, as chief of his community, also has significant social capital that encouraged people to go along with this foreign idea of hiking. Finally, Joseph's mother, Rosalyn, serves as an important bridge between the host families and Western hikers because of her three decades of experience cooking for Americans.

Doug and Austin Taylor contributed the concept for Expedition Ayiti by way of Doug's friend, Mike. The Taylors also tap technical expertise from their networks to create marketing materials for the enterprise, and they bring important social capital when negotiating new hiking routes with national leaders in Port au Prince.

Finally, the leadership team taps into the strengths of families in each village as they host the hikers. Leaders recognize that staying with host families is often a high point for Western hikers as they learn more about the culture and get to know people with very different lifestyles.

These assets combine to create a unique opportunity to empower the Haitians involved with this enterprise. Americans, according to Doug Taylor, feel guilty hiking through Haiti because they are not "helping" Haitians during their visit. But while there may be limited long-term material impact from one person's visit, viewed through an empowerment lens, the value of their presence is potentially very significant. Americans are paying money to be taught about the Haitian culture, to be introduced to and stay in the homes of Haitian people, and to see beautiful regions of the country. Their visit puts them in the role of learner, of submitting to another's cultural norms for a time. This certainly has the potential to be quite empowering for the hosts and their community.

PERSPECTIVES

What did you notice in this case?

How does Expedition Ayiti's approach differ from other social enterprises' approaches with which you are familiar?

Sixteen

IMON International

"We initiated the project but beyond that, for us,
it was important that it was a partnership.
It was a relationship of transferring knowledge,
of innovation, of resource sharing."

Sanavbar Sharipova

T ajikistan was a member of the Soviet Union from the
1920s until the disintegration of the Union in 1991.
Independence led to a civil war between communists
and an alliance of Islamic and democratic forces. By the mid-
1990s, tens of thousands of people had died from the fighting
and half a million people had been displaced. The war continued
sporadically until 1997 when a peace agreement was brokered,
and order began to return to the country. At that point, the
economy was very weak, and the country was largely dependent
on foreign aid.

Sanavbar Sharipova and Gulbahor Makhkamova were young professional women living through this crisis. In Sharipova's words,

> The 1990s were a very difficult time for everyone and especially for women who experienced a lot of violence and conflicts in the region. On top of that, people didn't have jobs. As we transformed from one system to another, people who usually worked for the government became unemployed. That was the situation for most of the people including myself and Gulbahor. We had both graduated—me from a Russian university, Gulbahor from a Tajik university. We experienced the same hardship as others experienced. We had families, children, and were thinking about what we could do.
>
> The first step was to organize people like us and create a network of women who could support each other and provide basic educational resources to others. We established this in 1995. The first training was for unemployed women who sat at home and didn't know what to do. They were depressed. They came from different fields—musicians, architects.
>
> The first training demonstrated a very big demand for women to get a new type of education and start up some type of activities. They got support from their families to establish enterprises. Some were home-based—bakeries, small shops. We worked very closely with the government to establish these. Later, we got involved with Mercy Corps. It was a very good relationship that we established with them.

THE PARTNERSHIP

Mercy Corps, along with several other NGOs, was working in Tajikistan during that time. Mercy Corps has first response teams around the world that meet urgent needs growing out of natural disasters, economic crises, and conflicts. Team members also stay to partner with communities for long-term recovery. According to Mercy Corps, "We're committed to creating global change through local impact – 84 percent of our team members are from the countries where they work."[113]

Sharipova continued,

> Mercy Corps provided support to further develop our training materials. In 1998, when we were together with Mercy Corps, we did a nation-wide survey among women to understand their needs. It was clear they needed financial resources if they were to apply their knowledge through starting a business. In 1998-1999, we started microcredit in the south of the country—business training and new loan activity.

In 1999, Mercy Corps and the National Association of Businesswomen of Tajikistan (NABWT), as the training group was called, together launched a lending arm and in 2005 the NABWT transitioned its lending arm into a for-profit microcredit lending organization, IMON International. (IMON means "hope" in Tajik.) Today, IMON International LLC is the largest microfinance institution in this Central Asian nation of 7.6 million people.

Gary Burniske was Mercy Corps' Country Director in Tajikistan from 2002 to 2006. His work with several humanitarian organizations and international public institutions over thirty-five years has taken him to nearly fifty countries in Africa, Asia, Latin America, and the former Soviet Union. I asked Burniske about his work with IMON International. In his words,

> Tajikistan was a new country and government institutions were weak. Regulations on banking and credit were non-existent. Mercy Corps was working with other groups

trying to construct institutions and help draft policy and legislation for there to be an environment that allowed businesses to develop and flourish.

Banks often had no idea how to lend to clients, to serve clients. Capital was not available for economic development. Capitalism was a dirty word. No small businesses existed. Sanavbar Sharipova and Gulbahor Makhkamova had a vision for helping women in business development to resolve poverty. One of the common businesses women wanted to start was hairdressing. They needed to have a business plan, needed to know where to locate the shop, who they would target as customers, which styles they'd specialize in …

These two women were very gregarious, movers and shakers. They were good at organizing women. They had a special touch that is very important in any business.

The women came back after the training saying, "This is great training, but we don't have the cash we need to start a business." Mercy Corps worked out an agreement with NABWT. We gave them $750,000 which was Mercy Corps money, and Mercy Corps retained ownership of the money in the beginning. It was a new environment, and the idea of microcredit was largely untested back in 1999.

NABWT invested that money in creating a loan portfolio. What they made off the loan interest they put back into the corpus, so they grew their loan portfolio and then took on more clients. The loan products that they developed had differing tiers. The lowest was the solidarity loan. A group of six to ten people, often members of the same community or a group of relatives, would come together to take out a loan under the name of the group.

I asked Sharipova to tell me about the lending groups. "Did the women know each other beforehand?"

Yes. It is the nature of the country and the program. When we started, we were working with tiny, small loans. They were not covered by guarantee or collateral. If something went wrong with one group member, others would help. Women needed to know and trust each other and monitor the discipline within the group. The group guarantee from the beginning worked very well. We had a very high level of repayment, and if one woman couldn't repay, the whole group repaid.

"How did you establish trust with these women?"

They came with expectations and dreams. When they were sitting in the training, they saw women [Gulbahor and I] who had the same issues as them. It was easier to establish trust in these relationships. I remember the days when we went to war-affected regions in the south. For hours they would be sharing their stories and their own family challenges.

"Gary, besides giving a grant that allowed NABWT to make loans, what else was Mercy Corps doing?"

Mercy Corps had technical advisors that provided NABWT with training, and with help setting up the loan systems. We also provided oversight as well as troubleshooting, problem-solving ... Institutional development is a key goal of ours, institutional capacity building. We see our role as transient.

Their road map then had them move from a microcredit lending organization to becoming an LLC. We developed an application, drew up statutes, and formed a new board of directors.

We also had partners in this process, including the Mennonite Economic Development Association, MEDA.

Mercy Corps wanted to include them in the work as well as some Tajiks from businesses and nonprofits.

LASTING IMPACT

"Gary, why do you believe IMON International succeeded when so many social enterprises fail?"

> Sanavbar Sharipova and Gulbahor Makhkamova were entrepreneurs. They understood it. They had their hearts in the right place socially. They were educated, and they had that entrepreneurial spirit. It was a combination of those things.
>
> Sanavbar is smooth, level-headed. The amount of pressure placed on them as we went through the ups and downs was tremendous. They were threatened to be thrown in jail, they had death threats. It was not easy.

I asked Sharipova for her perspective about IMON International's success as well.

> I think one of the key aspects of development was my vision for a long-lasting, sustainable institution, not one that would be in operation for a short period of time ... We have grown from a five-person staff to 1,700 employees serving more than 100,000 clients around the country.

"Sanavbar, what did Gary and others with Mercy Corps contribute most significantly?"

> We initiated the project, but beyond that, for us, it was important that it was a partnership. It was a relationship of transferring knowledge, of innovation, of resource sharing. We established a very unique relationship when

we were visiting the families of the people who came from the U.S. When we would travel to the capital, Dushanbe, [where Mercy Corps was based] they would meet us at the airport. It was very bad security. They would take us to their homes, provide food for us. They provided security for us as their family members. There were no hotels, so they were taking care of us as women from different parts. They stayed in our homes [when they traveled to see us.] We developed a very close personal relationship as well as a professional relationship.

We engaged in other relationships [through Mercy Corps] because once we established a relationship with one institution, they provided references to other institutions. That's how we got so much support—other partners who were from different parts of the country.

COMMENTARY

IMON International represents the strategic use of most of the unique assets Majority World leaders often hold (see the Complementary Assets Table in Chapter 13). Sharipova and Makhkamova had firsthand knowledge of what Tajik women were living through. They also had social capital as members of the community. As a result, the participants trusted Sharipova and Makhkamova, demonstrated not only by their decision to participate in the program but also by the personal stories they shared with the two leaders. More than two decades after the NABWT launched, it is easy to see that the two leaders had a long-term commitment to the project and patience that complimented their tenacity.

Considering assets the Americans had to offer, Mercy Corps, and Burniske in particular, brought entrepreneurial expertise as they collaborated on further developing the training manuals Sharipova and Makhkamova had written. Their technical skills and social capital were indispensable as government agreements were forged, loan systems were established, and even national laws were written. Finally, Mercy Corps not only provided financial capital for the microcredit institution but connected IMON International to others who provided capital as well.

Building an enterprise dependent on both Tajik and American assets required trust, mutual respect, and humility from every player. Burniske and the Mercy Corps expatriate team assumed that the micro-lending and business training would succeed or fail based on the creativity, skills, and drive of two Tajik women, not on what expats contributed to the team. Burniske's quick and confident response to my question about why IMON International succeeded reflects this. In his mind, the organization's sustainability and growth never depended on outsiders, but on the talent pool that existed inside the country.

In the same vein, every leader assumed they had to depend on each other to build the organization. Sharipova described leaders' strong personal relationships that bridged cultural differences. These were built on trust that grew out of extended time spent together. Leaders valued each other's strengths and recognized the need to be interdependent.

Finally, both Tajik and American leaders valued the assets brought by the women IMON International served. Sharipova and Burniske referred specifically to these women's professional skills, their discipline as they worked as members of lending groups, their courage, and their hope as they built a better future for themselves.

PERSPECTIVES

What did you notice in this case?

How does IMON International's approach differ from other social enterprises' approaches with which you are familiar?

Seventeen

Floral

*"What keeps us going is seeing the impact and positive
changes the money is bringing to the community—
children going to school because their fees can be paid,
improvements of shelter, new buildings being built."*

Penelope Gebeda

F loral [a pseudonym] is a social enterprise with a
different kind of partnership than those described
in the previous three chapters, but one in which the
value of multiple players' assets shines through again. In this
African country, farmland has been a key issue in violent
racial struggles. Several years ago, the government started
seizing property from white farmers and giving it to black
citizens as compensation for the abuses of colonial rule.
But agricultural outputs began to stall because the white
landowners possessed the agricultural expertise.

PARTNERING

In 2011, David Smith [a pseudonym], a white man, experienced this land seizure. After twenty years of legally owning his land following Independence, he was told to leave. Samuel Gebeda [a pseudonym], a black owner of significant farmland, lived nearby and asked Smith to bring his workers and what he could carry to his farm. Gebeda's daughter, Penelope [a pseudonym], had just finished her university degree and started working with Smith. According to Penelope Gebeda,

> I had book knowledge but absolutely no practical farming knowledge. David became my mentor and my teacher. Our farm was not productive at that time—my family was just getting our farm running again. We were all starting over.
>
> David started to farm with us after 20 years of running his own farm. He had been growing flower seeds since the late 1980s. Together we started an outgrower contract flower seed scheme in the rural area. We were bringing a cash crop with a difference to smallholder rural farmers.
>
> He has been through so much being kicked off his farm. He had the contract to grow the flower seeds for Holland. It was his idea to try outgrowing with the rural farmers. We used David's contacts and farming knowledge to support farmers as they developed their own businesses.

Holland has one growing season, and the demand for seeds from the U.S, China, and other major importers outstrips the Dutch company's ability to supply. Gebeda and Smith sell seeds to local farmers who have two growing seasons. Floral employees train and support the farmers as they grow the flowers and work with them when they process the flowers in the farmers' fields. Floral then sells the seeds to the company in the Netherlands.

Penelope Gebeda continued,

They are characterized as subsistence farmers—they grow food for consumption—so they don't have money for health care, education, and clothes. Floral uses the skills a farmer already has, his basic technology, and his basic need to uplift to make him better.

We encourage farmers to use what they have—no insecticide—so their food crops are not endangered. Just weed it in the same way. We're using the practices they use with their other crops so it's compatible with what they grow. We're giving them a cash crop so they're not compromising their food crop. We say, "Just the way you weed your maize, weed the flowers and keep them clean." We encourage them to use manure, composting, rather than use what little resources they have to go buy inorganic fertilizer, which is quite expensive.

We do training and evaluation to be sure farmers are successful in growing 40 to 50 kilograms of seed from one kilogram of seed. Every month we visit them to be sure they are doing well.

"I understand there are farmers waiting to work with you."

We are limited by demand for the seeds that limits the number of growers we can contract every year. To keep growing, we are looking for other crops to introduce that are not limited by our market. Honey is one possibility. Also, capacity. We only have so many people now who can visit the farms each month.

We started with forty growers. In three years, we had 200 growers. We have a waiting list of 200 growers wanting to grow seed in an area with 2,500 farmers. I've only reached 8 percent of the market with 200 farmers. It's the same with others who work in other regions of the country. We don't have a problem with competition because so little of the farm market is tapped now.

"How are you growing the business?"

It's through word of mouth. Next door neighbors have come and seen the change in the livelihoods, and they have wanted to grow our seed. We have grouped our farmers into geographical areas. In each group we have a group leader. They wanted to evaluate themselves, and it creates a natural competition between groups to see who grows the best flowers, who gets the best seed. That motivates and encourages them, and it also spreads the word in the community.

"What impact have you seen from Floral's work?"

We are not only providing a cash crop to our growers. We are also providing knowledge on conservation farming practices that will benefit the other crops they grow. They are increasing their yields at the same time they are improving their soils.

COMMENTARY

Why is Floral flourishing? As with the previous three cases, its approach that taps multiple assets has proven powerful. Smith is not American, but he formerly represented the ruling class and as such shares several things in common with Americans. He brings entrepreneurial expertise, agricultural expertise, and global contacts to Floral. Gebeda brings her formal agricultural knowledge, an understanding of how to empower vulnerable people, and an important measure of trust with small farmers, even though she comes from a different social class. Both she and Smith have a long-term commitment to the farmers' development and patience as they have allowed word of mouth to expand the enterprise.

Both leaders also highly value the farmers' assets. They demonstrated respect for the farmers by building on the skills they already had. They consciously decided to use the freely available natural resources rather than introduce expensive innovations such as inorganic fertilizer from the outside. Gebeda and Smith also recognized the asset of the farmers' communities in this collectivist culture. Patiently letting the first Floral farmers succeed and share their story with others has resulted in a waiting list of 200 people. It has also empowered the farmers as they made their own decision whether to join the enterprise without outside pressure.

Finally, humility plays a central role in Floral. The Gebedas could have simply watched Smith leave the area, but despite the country's colonial history, they invited him and his workers onto their land and offered to work with him. Smith, for his part, possessed intellectual, social, and financial capital. During a very unsettling time in his own life, he made the decision to invest this capital in helping subsistence farmers grow a cash crop that could greatly increase their standard of living.

PERSPECTIVES

What did you notice in this case?

How does Floral's approach differ from other social enterprises' approaches with which you are familiar?

Eighteen

Global Mamas

*"We focus on the needs of our employees
and what they are requesting....
We care for them in community."*

Alice Grau

Global Mamas was founded in 2003 when six Ghanaian women partnered with two former Peace Corps volunteers to establish what was initially called Women in Progress. At the time, the two Americans, both of whom have MBAs, were providing business and financial management consulting to Ghanaians through the recently launched Women's Cooperative Bank in Ghana.

THE BEGINNING

Patience Essibu, Global Mama's People Development Manager, described the enterprise's beginning this way:

> It was due to research. When we went around meeting amazing, dynamic women in Ghana, they told us if we teach them how to manage their businesses but don't find markets outside Ghana for them, there will be no businesses left to manage.

The eight women shared a vision of transforming the lives of women entrepreneurs in Ghana by supporting them as they grew their businesses. As they explain on their website,

> The Mamas achieve prosperity by creating and selling unique, handcrafted products of the highest quality. Being able to do the work they love and being empowered by financial independence leads to greater happiness. They realize their dreams of having the opportunity to support their families, send their children to school, improve their health, and save for the future.

According to Alice Grau, Creative Director for Global Mamas,

> All of this was founded on real friendship, real relationships. There was back and forth and dialogue. It wasn't the Americans saying, "I've got this thing, and I'm going to bring this to you." The Ghanaian women instead said, "The training is great, but we can see [help with finding new markets for our products] benefitting us more." It's always been this way [with Global Mamas]. It's always been very participatory. We are all global mamas. The success of this is for all of us.

Today Global Mamas produces hundreds of items in seven locations around Ghana, including batik textile products, recycled glass beads, and shea butter. Much of the product is shipped to the United States for sale, some to Europe, and some is sold in shops in Ghana's capital, Accra. They currently employ or contract with 360 people.

What is one of the most important decisions they have made? Grau believes it is this:

We manage everything from product to shipping. We are connected from artisan to end consumer. Vertical integration makes the job something the locals are part of. It integrates them into many levels.

Each year we have a design competition where we engage mamas from all our locations. We pay the mama who wins for the rights to her print. She gets top billing as the producer for that print and, depending on its popularity, we may train others to make it as well.

We also contract with leaders called "madams" who the other women look up to because of their confidence and leadership abilities. There is still that colonial mindset, so it's important to have women who are bold enough and can lead by setting an example for others that they too have skills and innovative ideas to offer. These madams are identified in the communities in which they work or gradually take on that role as they are empowered and gain confidence in the organization. When they talk about goals and dreams, a lot of them say they want to train more women so they can have work. We help them do that. They may employ ten women and take on apprentices and other employees depending on their capacity or space.

Over the years, the organization has added a Boutique Manager, Human Resource Manager, Quality Manager, and

Jewelry Manager, all of whom are Ghanaian and all of whom rose through Global Mama's Quality Control Program. Today, there are only three Western employees in Ghana. The enterprise's impact through opening new possibilities for women across Ghana is significant. From the influence of the madams throughout the country, to the organizational leadership roles several women now hold, to the girls who can attend school because of the mamas' incomes, the ripple effects are substantial.

ASSETS

I asked Grau and Essibu about the most valuable assets the Ghanaians and Americans bring to the organization. Essibu responded,

> Americans have the technical know-how. Also, having a Western interest, a Western face helps a lot. That's how countries go. They know the requirements of Americans. They are a good business arm for the end-user. We try to incorporate the two quarters together to achieve synergy.
>
> [With regard to the Ghanaians' assets], it becomes simple for the mamas to communicate with the African leaders. They see us as part of them, and they understand us more and we understand them more. We understand the language so we can communicate well. Sometimes it becomes hard to understand when an expat tries to communicate.

Grau added,

> Cultural understanding. No matter how long Kristin and Renae [the co-founders] have been there, whatever we ask, Ghanaians will do. Even now it's, "Yes, Madam." Ghanaian leaders bring connections. Patience [Essibu] speaks the language.

She has been with us since the beginning. She and Renae have been in the office when there was no office. They were sleeping on the floor. There was no bathroom. She knows the culture of the organization.

All the sites are now run by Ghanaian managers. Ten years ago, they were all run by Westerners. Each person brought new ideas, which is valuable, but it can also disrupt things. A Ghanaian manager brings cultural understanding, stability. She can have conversations that a producer might not be comfortable having with us.

> Besides their skills and expertise, they bring cultural competency. We can't truly understand the culture because we weren't raised Ghanaian.

Grau also addressed the topic of Americans' unique contributions to the enterprise:

> Market access. It's the ability to communicate with the culture on the American side. These are the products we have. Fine-tuning—this is beautiful artwork that is made in Ghana. Keeping it true to art but also understanding quality expectations and the trends of markets here.
>
> We seek feedback on our business, set goals, seek insight from outsiders. We bring that perspective. We need to systematize. We need to use a standard size set for clothing, standard grade rules. These are skills I was trained on through work at Sears and Kmart.

Regarding leaders' relationships with their employees, Grau observed,

> We focus on the needs of our employees and what they are requesting. We partner with them on what sort of training they would like and try to provide those things

that would really help them to be better businesswomen and moms. Most of the mamas, as we call our business partners, have craft skills. Global Mamas enhances their skills through hands-on training in advanced techniques, quality improvement, and creative design.

We also offer training in finance and bookkeeping. Our biggest request from the employees was health and English training. In talking with them, we see what is important to them. By being grassroots, we gain a more holistic view. They view being happy and healthy as key.

We care for them in the community. We have hosted a cleanup in a big market. We do health training on cancer and empower them as businesspeople and as women with a voice. The training is unique to each community based on what the women want.

I asked Essibu about the best aspects of being a Global Mama.

Being able to see women become more confident. Doing significant things that even someone going to school could not do, like being able to support their family and extended family, growing their business, saving for future expansion, and developing themselves.

How do they evaluate the organization? Grau described the following approach:

We focus on empowerment. Every year we talk about how the women's businesses have changed. Have they acquired new equipment? Are they saving money? How many children are they sending to school? Often, they are not just sending their children, but nieces and nephews as well. Last year the mamas sent 217 children to school— and only half of them were their biological children.

We ask questions about their health, their family's health, what new is happening in their lives. We ask about their emotions, how they are feeling, what the money situation looks like.

COMMENTARY

As with the previous four cases, the Ghanaian leaders of Global Mamas have brought crucial social capital at the local level, building teams of artisans, and acting as mentors to them. They have used their knowledge of the culture to structure an organization that reflects Ghanaian values, and they exhibit patience and long-term commitment as they holistically build into the mamas. Many leaders have also brought knowledge of what it is to be poor as well as knowledge of the required artisan skills.

The Americans, for their part, have contributed business expertise and market access as they sell the products in multiple countries around the world. Together, the Ghanaian and American leaders have employed several strategies for empowering the mamas, including using "madams," promoting from within, and caring holistically for employees. Finally, the mamas themselves have contributed to the organization through their skills, their determination, and their identification of the training they most need to flourish.

PERSPECTIVES

What did you notice in this case?

How does Global Mamas' approach differ from other social enterprises' approaches with which you are familiar?

Nineteen

Three Key Assumptions

"Relationships are based on four principles:
respect, understanding, acceptance, and appreciation."

Mahatma Gandhi

The social enterprises described in Chapters 14 through 18 benefit from full participation by the nationals on the leadership teams. They also benefit from support by the intended benefactors. They are growing enterprises, and they are helping to bring about positive change in people's lives. How did leaders achieve these positive results when so many enterprises have failed by one definition or another? I noted three primary assumptions that drive their work. These assumptions are particularly significant because they are consistent with key ideas the Majority World leaders interviewed for this study emphasized again and again:

- Our enterprise must emphasize empowerment.
- Employees and customers are members of important community systems that must not be ignored.
- We must recognize our personal limitations.

This chapter explores how leaders of these five social enterprises acted upon each of these assumptions.

1. OUR ENTERPRISE MUST EMPHASIZE EMPOWERMENT.

Leaders operationalized this assumption in multiple ways:

- Using local resources to build the business
- Engaging local people in defining the problem that needed to be solved
- Providing training and skill-building opportunities
- Assuming the local people held essential resources
- Securing regular, honest feedback
- Getting proximate

Leaders operationalized empowerment first by relying on local natural resources. Expedition Ayiti used the beauty of the land and existing trails, Aqua Clara International used only locally available materials, and Floral used farmers' land and natural fertilizers. The emphasis was not on introducing outside innovations but creative, more effective use of local resources that the people already possessed or could easily access.

A second approach to empowerment involved asking local people to help define the problem to be solved. For example, Aqua Clara International asked communities to determine when or if they needed safer water and IMON International began providing microcredit, in addition to training, based on survey results of women's articulated needs.

Third, enterprise leaders provided training for the local people they hoped to help. For example, Expedition Ayiti trained the hosts and Global Mamas specifically asked the mamas what training they most wanted. But more than that, leaders also assumed those they were trying to help brought essential resources to the enterprise. To cite just a few examples, IMON International tapped the enthusiasm, resiliency, strength, and existing skills of the women in their programs. Global Mamas used women's artisan skills and assumed mamas would accurately assess their own training needs. Aqua Clara International relied on local leaders' training skills as well as the trust these leaders already enjoyed with others in their community. Expedition Ayiti built the enterprise around local people's deep knowledge of the region's geography and culture as well as their hospitality, while Floral built upon farmers' existing agricultural knowledge to help them increase their income.

Finally, leaders secured regular feedback from their customers and employees. Global Mamas gathered feedback about the artisans' satisfaction with the enterprise as measured by their willingness to encourage other women to join. IMON International regularly solicited feedback about the women's concerns and needs.

These efforts all point to an overarching approach that prioritized proximity. Leaders built relationships with those they wanted to help by sharing their lives with them and working alongside them.

Thinking back to Majority World and American differences in problem definition discussed in Chapter 8, these enterprises focused on increasing material resources *and* empowering the people they wanted to help. They pursued big goals *and* simultaneously pursued relationships with the people they were trying to support. They committed tremendous effort to their work *and* assumed it would take a long time to build something that brought about positive, sustained change. In sum, these teams blended culturally different approaches as they built their enterprises.

2. EMPLOYEES AND CUSTOMERS ARE MEMBERS OF IMPORTANT COMMUNITY SYSTEMS THAT MUST NOT BE IGNORED.

Leaders of these five enterprises assumed they were working with strong communities of people as much as they were working with individuals. They operated from this assumption in three concrete ways:

- Building trust with community leaders
- Tapping the social capital of local organizations such as schools, churches, and local governments
- Assuming if the enterprise had value, word-of-mouth would engage people with it

First, members of the enterprises conveyed respect for community leaders and engaged them in their work. For example, the Aqua Clara International team initially listened to local leaders as they articulated the needs of their communities and then worked with them to find solutions. Global Mamas employed madams, women who were already respected members of their communities, to serve as models and business leaders for the younger women.

The enterprises also tapped the strengths of intact groups. IMON International utilized groups of relatives and friends as they provided training and formed lending groups, knowing that these women already had strong bonds with each other. Aqua Clara International built relationships with school leaders, who typically were trusted members of the community.

Leaders also used the collectives to spread the word about their idea. Aqua Clara International used community launches led by local leaders to introduce their products and relied on word of mouth as their only marketing tool. Similarly, Floral let the farmers sell the opportunity to grow flower seeds to their family and friends. Floral knew that trust already existed among the farmers, so if seed growers encouraged others to join the enterprise, they likely would.

American leaders could have naturally focused on the individual as they built these enterprises. Instead, the cross-cultural leadership teams took account of the cultures in which they were working and shifted their approach to one that tapped the strengths of collectivist societies.

3. WE MUST RECOGNIZE OUR PERSONAL LIMITATIONS.

The third assumption that guided each of these five teams relates to assets. From the very start, leaders believed they had to tap others' assets if they were going to build a sustainable enterprise. They operationalized this assumption in two ways:

- Recognizing the value of a person who could act as a cultural bridge
- Tapping the assets of multiple people for the leadership team

First, whether it was intentional or not, several of the teams included someone who served as a bridge between the two cultures represented in the group, a cultural translator. Paul Nelson, retired CEO of the Crowell Trust, spoke to the power of a third culture person:

Expats understand the culture like nationals can't. It's like asking a fish to describe what water feels like. They know no other. Local people don't know about local hotels because they've never needed one. In the same way, they don't know what it's like to be a foreigner trying to navigate governmental red tape. That's where an expatriate can be so valuable.

Put in terms of a cultural dimension described in Chapter 5, these leadership teams included someone who had developed the ability to translate high-context communication for low-context individuals. For example, Gary Burniski with Mercy Corps had spent decades living in Majority World countries. His understanding of cross-cultural dynamics played a key role in building IMON International, successfully working with the Tajik government, and bringing other NGOs into the work.

Doug Taylor, with Expedition Ayiti, had lived in Haiti for two years and had traveled there multiple times since moving back to the United States. He had developed a deep understanding of the culture and fluency in the language which allowed him to build a long-term friendship, and ultimately a business partnership, with Gerald Joseph.

Likewise, the two Americans who helped found Global Mamas had spent years living in Ghana as Peace Corps volunteers, building an understanding of the culture as well as friendships with people in the region. It was through these friendships that a Ghanaian eventually articulated the idea for Global Mamas, and the organization was born.

These leaders opened themselves up to the vulnerabilities that come with learning another language, developing cross-cultural friendships, and living as members of a foreign culture. They no doubt made mistakes in the process, but these mistakes helped them build the requisite trust and respect that allowed them to co-lead these enterprises.

On a side note, the careful reader may recognize that most of the people who are cited multiple times throughout the pages of this book acted as cultural translators during the interviews. Some are Americans who have spent extended time living in other countries. Others are Majority World citizens who have lived for an extended period in the United States. Their insights were invaluable as I wrote this book.

In addition to having cultural translators on the teams, the enterprise leaders assumed they alone did not have all the assets needed to build a successful enterprise. They needed people who brought different skills, different forms of social capital, and different perspectives to the work.

IMON International is a powerful example of combining the vision, skills, and social capital of local leaders with the business skills and financial capital of Americans. Floral is similar in that the black farmer had agricultural skills as well as social capital with the people she hoped to engage, while the white farmer had access to international markets along with business and agricultural skills. Finally, Aqua Clara International leaders recognized the value of their technical skills as well as their limitations as business builders and marketers. They, therefore, partnered with local entrepreneurs who marketed the filters as they saw fit, trained new users, and provided follow-up support to them. The respect leaders had for each other was evident throughout the interviews. The table below highlights these findings.

Three Key Perspectives

Emphasize Empowerment
- Use local resources to build the business
- Engage local people in defining the problem
- Provide training and skill-building opportunities
- Assume the local people hold essential resources
- Secure regular, honest feedback
- Get proximate

Engage with Community Systems
- Build trust with community leaders
- Tap the social capital of local organizations
- Assume word-of-mouth will attract people

Embrace Your Personal Limitations
- Include a cultural bridge
- Tap multiple asset sets

This value of tapping multiple assets is consistent with Western-based research findings on diversity. Teams that are racially, ethnically, and gender diverse tend to be more innovative due not only to the new information members offer to the group, but also because interacting with people who are different encourages all members to prepare more for meetings, to expect varied viewpoints, and to anticipate that reaching consensus will take effort.[114, 115] Diverse groups are also more likely to constantly reevaluate facts and to process new information more carefully, which may lead to better decision-making as well.[116]

Previous chapters have examined the value of cross-cultural partnerships from multiple angles. The remainder of this chapter considers the value that having multiple skill sets and both males and females on the leadership teams provided to these five social enterprises.

TAPPING THE STRENGTHS OF MULTIPLE SKILL SETS

In the 1950s, John Holland concluded that our vocational choices reflect our personality preferences. Ultimately his research led him to divide the world of work into six categories, each with distinctives and strengths that reflect the personalities who enjoy that type of work. Every person tends to prefer one category, although we are usually a combination of two or three categories. The diagram that follows describes these six types.

Holland's World of Work

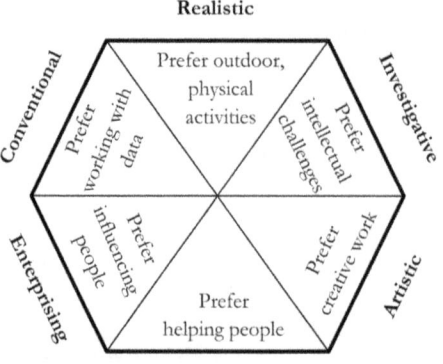

As I interviewed people from these five enterprises, I heard voices from each of these categories. First, there were the *Social* voices who were focused primarily on the individual and his or her needs. They had made a long-term commitment to providing direct services to others, they invested their lives in a cause, and they engaged with their whole selves. They knew the local language, had built relationships with the local people, and had generally worked to understand and value the local culture. Many of the women with Global Mamas may be examples of people strong in the Social category. Building the enterprise was certainly relational and long-term, and leaders reflected a strong desire to help women by carefully listening to them and offering services that addressed their top priorities.

There were the *Artistic* types who were imaginative, creative, and very sensitive to the world around them. Leaders within Global Mamas, particularly designers and the artisans themselves, likely had aspects of the artistic category in their profile as well.

Others identified primarily with the *Investigative* realm. They were drawn to solving scientific problems through observation and analysis. They were very comfortable in a lab, working for long periods on a complex intellectual challenge such as building low-cost filters for contaminated water using only local resources.

The *Realistic* types loved being out in the field, working with farmers, or hiking across Haiti with groups of Americans.

There were also the *Conventional* types, often filling financial, accounting, and other support roles for enterprises. They were typically not in the spotlight, enjoying instead the work of keeping an organization fiscally sound and perhaps keeping leaders who had an affinity for risk from making decisions that could jeopardize the organization.

Finally, there were *Enterprising* people—individuals who were gifted in influencing, persuading, and managing others. They tended to move fast, exude enthusiasm and confidence, and take risks. Leaders with IMON International in particular seemed to have these strengths.

These five teams reflected professional diversity among their leaders. However, during the interviews for this book, it was easy to identify other social enterprises that had not tapped into adequate professional diversity as they launched. For example, there were cases where Investigative types had developed a technology, but they lacked an Enterprising person with an understanding of how to build a business around it. There were cases of strategic business models being developed by an Enterprising person, but the model failing because there was no Social person on the leadership team who truly understood the people and had strong relationships with them. Finally, there were cases where a Social person with a heart to help a community had launched an enterprise, but it failed because he or she did not have someone on the team who knew how to build a sustainable business. In this study, the professional diversity of each leadership team proved highly valuable.

TAPPING GENDER DIFFERENCES

In addition to professional diversity, research on leadership also points to the value of teams that include both men and women. These teams enjoy the benefit of a greater variety of perspectives which in turn strengthens the overall performance of the enterprise.[117, 118, 119]

The results these five social enterprises have produced support these findings. Aqua Clara International has generally used male American scientists and female sales and support people in the field; Floral is a partnership between a man and a woman; IMON International involved an American male and two Tajik females leading the work; Expedition Ayiti includes American and Haitian men leading marketing and logistics while a woman provides hosts with cooking and hospitality training.

As I interviewed the leaders of these four cases, they did not speak specifically about the value of having both men and women on the team. However, that topic did surface several times as I interviewed teams that did not have this diversity. Alice Grau of Global Mamas, an enterprise led exclusively by women, described a significant challenge they had faced, which perhaps reflected an absence of more achievement- than relationally-oriented men on their leadership team:

> We tried to employ every woman without really giving them dignified work. We struggled and still do struggle to have that healthy balance between owning a business and wanting to also operate more like an NGO to help everyone we possibly can. We have found ourselves in the habit of creating roles for people because we wanted them to stick around. However, it doesn't do anyone any good if we accept bad products and are not focused on quality and improvement because the business won't grow, and the skills of the women will never improve.

Two other female-led enterprises in this study also struggled because leaders tried to nurture people but put their businesses at risk in the process. For example, the female CEO of an enterprise that supplies gifts from around the world to North American markets shared one of the challenges she has faced. "I invested too much in some groups and did not drop them soon enough because I wanted to help. There needs to be a balance." According to Hofstede's research on cultural differences, this emphasis on relationships, harmony, and caring for others is more typical of females.

On the other end of the continuum, an enterprise led by several men and only one woman, all American, focused instead on the masculine cultural values of achievement and expansion. This enterprise is built around a technology designed for use in rural Sub-Saharan Africa. The men focused on distributing the new technology as broadly and as quickly as possible while Mary Durby [not her real name] emphasized building trust and respect with potential users. She described her unique contribution this way:

Africans got to have input as to how training [for using the technology] played out. In each country, we had people on the ground training and connecting with local officials. They saw the vision of what it could be. Nationals put in long hours to make this work.

I planned the workshops and had national partners involved with putting it on. Africans were part of the agenda for each workshop. It was not just me doing the training. The local people we worked with are so creative. So, in several countries, we had a team of Africans doing the workshops, and I was the only Westerner and the only woman who was part of the training team.

As I worked in Africa, I developed friendships with several of the people. When I go back, I stay in their homes. I realize that is rare for Americans to do, especially for men, but it's wonderful. No man on our team has ever had that happen.

Mary successfully built interdependent relationships with the local people that were based on trust and mutual respect. These relationships, she believes, were essential if people were going to invest in the innovation. The male leaders did not, however, value Mary's unique contribution, seeing it as unnecessary and time-consuming. According to Mary, they were interested in press releases and sales numbers they could quote rather than the individuals they were trying to help. Significant friction has ensued over the years between Mary and the male members of the leadership team as a result.

Gender-diverse teams bring value to an organization. They also provide important opportunities for women to lead in locations where they have traditionally filled only limited and particularly vulnerable roles in society. This leadership model has the power to shape not only an entire community's perspective about women but also people's views for generations to come.

CONCLUSIONS

Consistent with published research, these five social enterprises point to the value of teams that include men and women; business, technical, creative, and helping-oriented people; and people from different cultural backgrounds. Leaders of these organizations recognized their own strengths and skills while also intuitively sensing their limitations. They assumed they needed others' assets if they were going to offer truly valuable opportunities to vulnerable people.

They did not stop there, however. They also tapped both human and natural resources that were available locally as well as the power of local groups and institutions such as schools and neighborhoods.

The success of these five enterprises in terms of buy-in from those they were intended to serve, continued growth, and the positive change they are bringing about in people's lives is not coincidental. Both national and American leaders recognized their own limitations and blended a diverse teams' invaluable assets into their enterprise's DNA from the very beginning.

PERSPECTIVES

Do you agree with the three key assumptions detailed in this chapter? Why or why not?

To what extent do you believe these assumptions are also relevant when building an enterprise with leaders from a marginalized population in the United States?

Which of the eleven bulleted approaches in the Three Key Perspectives table seem most powerful to you?

Regular evaluation that includes both employees and customers is an essential aspect of building a sustainable social enterprise. *Do you agree with this statement? Why or why not?*

Twenty

Impediments to Partnership

"Culture hides more than it reveals and strangely enough what it hides, it hides most effectively from its own participants. Years of study have convinced me that the real job is not to understand foreign culture but to understand our own."

Edward T. Hall

The previous chapter answers a "what" question. For the social enterprises in this study that were based upon cross-cultural partnerships, what approaches helped them build sustainable businesses that were attractive to the local people they wanted to support and brought about positive change?

This chapter focuses on answering a "why" question. Why are partnerships generally counterintuitive, countercultural, and seemingly counterproductive, particularly for Americans? Several I interviewed identified three influences that they believe fight against Americans' perceived need to partner. The first two ideas are fairly straight forward to describe. The third is far more nuanced.

THE MEDIA

In interviews, people spoke of the powerful role the media can play in shaping entrepreneurs' perceptions. Gerald Joseph with Expedition Ayiti commented, "There is so much bad news about the country, but we want to make sure to show them that the country is not as bad as they show in the news." Laud Basing, a Ghanaian microbiologist and social entrepreneur, lived for several years in the United States as he worked as a postdoctoral fellow. He observed this:

> Americans feel like they must help based on how American media portrays other people. I've been here in the U.S. for a while. When I watch the news, sometimes I'm like, "They portray Africa as just one place and as a place where there is a lot of poverty, disease, and war." So, I tell people that yes, there is poverty in Africa, but there is poverty in the U.S. as well.
>
> Second, the media portrays a lot of disease in Africa— HIV, malaria. [The story the media tells is that] it is common to have conditions there.
>
> And then there is the conflict the media portrays. Yes, there are wars in Africa, but when you look at Africa as just one country it's not an accurate picture. Just like looking at the U.S.— some areas are more peaceful than others. That is how Africa is, too. We need to be able to continue comparing with scenarios that are occurring in the U.S.
>
> There are a lot of backward people who have nothing to do. This is a fourth way the media portrays Africans. I have a PhD in microbiology. People look at me funny when I tell them that. They do not see how I could be so educated that I could come to the U.S. to work.

To the extent that American media portrays weak and almost helpless Majority World societies, American entrepreneurs are unlikely to value the strengths that exist among the people there. It is easy to see why these entrepreneurs would assume the people are candidates for rescue rather than collaboration.

DOMESTIC AND FOREIGN POLICY

Others I interviewed perceived a tendency within the federal government to elevate American purposes and American good above that of other countries. As one American who had lived in the Majority World for decades commented, "The 2016 election exemplified this. We are going to do it our way, and we are going to accomplish our purposes. We are going to make America great again."

An East African living in the United States agreed. "Very few people and countries think that America wants to help them. They think that America advances her own interests. They don't care about others."

This person also observed that domestic policy does not always value American lives equally either. "They don't care about the dignity of the human being. I do not see people valuing life as much here [in the United States]. How you exclude people from government support, for example. Your policies and laws don't always value life." These perceptions depict a society that is powerful yet limited in its desire to empower the most vulnerable, whether at home or abroad.

HEROISM

The desire to be a hero was a third barrier to partnering and empowering others that surfaced multiple times in the interviews. An American social entrepreneur working in East Africa observed,

There's definitely a hero status generated around an individual. Their status sort of overwhelms the work the social enterprise is doing. The celebrity situation is interesting. I saw it at SOCAP [Social Capital Markets] a lot. Any space, once you get behind the scenes, it's more political than you expect.

An Indian social entrepreneur also reflected on the hero mentality she had observed among both Americans and Indians:

In social enterprise, the founder is a hero figure. But that person's gains never trickle down because financial gains, in particular, are not the main issue. They're not what others are looking for. There's nothing that the larger team works toward. It's all about the hero. It's like a hero-driven organization. There isn't a rule book. There's no moral compass.

Sometimes the hero status is more subtle. An American-led social enterprise that many readers would be familiar with intentionally did not create an exit plan. When I asked why, a leader explained,

Our plan was communicated very clearly from the start— we are here to stay—but the locals didn't believe it. They are very fearful of groups leaving. They don't want [our organization] to fail.

What will happen when they leave? How much money will stop flowing? What if we have a bad harvest? They've seen others leave and things fall apart. They didn't necessarily want an exit strategy—they hadn't seen a lot of good come from that.

This organization has a desire to help that seems to be grounded in healthy motives, but is it also grounded in an assumption that serving as a community's savior is the best long-term approach to development?

David Edson, an American social entrepreneur who grew up in India, observed this hero mentality as well. "You always have kids from the States in pictures with twenty African kids, talking about what an amazing thing they did. When I worked internationally, we dubbed them Poverty Safaris. Come in, take pictures, go home."

Americans' cultural bent toward optimism, moving fast, and individualism likely contributes to this tendency toward heroism rather than an emphasis on empowering others. It is important to understand that this perspective is embedded in our history. Following is an excerpt from "Manifest Destiny," a newspaper article written by John O'Sullivan in 1845:

> [O]ur national birth was the beginning of a new history, the formation, and progress of an untried political system, which separates us from the past and connects us with the future only; and so far as regards to the entire development of the natural rights of man, in moral, political, and national life, we confidently assume that our country is destined to be the great nation of futurity....
>
> Yes, we are the nation of progress, of individual freedom, of universal enfranchisement.... For this blessed mission to the nations of the world, which are shut out from the life-giving light of truth, has America been chosen; and her high example shall smite unto death the tyranny of kings, hierarchs, and oligarchs, and carry the glad tidings of peace and goodwill where myriads now endure an existence scarcely more enviable than that of beasts of the field. Who, then, can doubt that our country is destined to be the great nation of futurity?[120]

The words seem horribly arrogant to us now, but how much distance exists between these ideas and what many Americans deeply believe today about our superior example on a host of issues, especially when shaped by the media's portrayal of Majority World countries? How many Americans believe we must heroically address these issues in other countries if we are to experience a more just world?

Stan Nussbaum wrote a book for international students who are trying to understand and engage successfully with American culture. He reflected on what can become a dangerous facet of Americans' vision for the world:

> We have built a nation that has become the global center of economic and military power. We imagine, rightly or wrongly, that if our influence could become even stronger throughout the world, the effect would be good for everyone, not just for us. Oppressive rulers would be replaced by responsible ones. Civil wars would stop. Women would be treated with dignity. Poverty would decline. On the other hand, if nations do not welcome American influence and American values, we are not optimistic about their futures.[121]

American social enterprise organizations at times support this heroic approach as well. For example, Ashoka looks for the following qualities in the people it takes on as Fellows:

- A truly new idea for solving a public need
- Creativity both in vision/goal setting and in problem-solving
- Entrepreneurial quality—driven by their vision
- An idea that is likely to solve an important social problem at the national level or beyond
- The ethical fiber of the individual[122]

It is interesting to note the extent to which this list reflects the American cultural values of innovation, drive, and an individualistic approach to social enterprise. Little emphasis is placed on empowering practices such as interdependence, recognition of the entrepreneur's limitations, or valuing of local resources.

To cite a second example, the Skoll Foundation presents the annual Skoll Awards for Social Entrepreneurship. As recently as 2020 their criteria for the award included the following:

- Social Entrepreneur – The organization is led by a visionary social entrepreneur whose values are embedded in the culture of the organization.
- Impact Potential – The organization's innovation is positioned to effect large-scale policy, behavior, and/or infrastructure/systems change and shows evidence of significant impact already achieved.
- Collaboration – The organization has partnerships in place to optimize its model and execute its mission on a larger scale. It is a key factor that has local, regional, national, and/or other key players in its ecosystem.
- Innovation – The organization has an approach that fundamentally disrupts an unsustainable and unjust equilibrium to solve social and/or environmental problems.[123]

Like Ashoka, Skoll emphasizes innovation, having a clear vision, and being driven by this vision. Skoll Award recipients also usually have a sound business model that is scalable as well as strong, strategic partnerships. These partnerships, however, may have quite different characteristics than the partnerships in the five cases I studied.

For example, Sarah Zak Borgman, The Skoll Foundation's Director of Community and Convenings, observed,

Many philanthropic organizations, including Skoll, have taken a deeper look at how to support the inner well-being of organizational leaders at a time when fatigue and burn-out could undermine their critical work. We must take good care of those who take care of the most marginalized and excluded.[124]

"Taking care" of people seems to place social entrepreneurs in the role of hero or savior, rather than as only one player within a system that includes multiple people's assets and is focused on empowering the most vulnerable.

A COLLABORATIVE APPROACH

David Bornstein, in his book *How to Change the World: Social Entrepreneurs and the Power of New Ideas*,[125] offered a different Western perspective on the ideal characteristics of a social entrepreneur, based on a study he had found. In his words,

It is commonly assumed that highly successful entrepreneurs are more confident and persistent than most others, including less successful entrepreneurs. This may not be true: One of the most intriguing papers I came across contrasted the behavior of highly successful and average entrepreneurs…. The most successful entrepreneurs were the ones most determined to achieve a long-term goal that was deeply meaningful to them…. They were more concerned with quality and efficiency and more committed to the people they employed and engaged with in business or as partners. Finally, they valued long-term considerations over short-term gain.

Bornstein cited a study by David C. McClelland titled, "Characteristics of Successful Entrepreneurs"[126] that identified the following:

1. Willingness to self-correct
2. Willingness to share credit
3. Willingness to break free of established structures
4. Willingness to cross disciplinary boundaries
5. Willingness to work quietly
6. A strong ethical impetus

Humility, willingness to self-correct (especially based on regular feedback), utilizing knowledge from various disciplines, sharing credit—these attributes are much more consistent with my findings. It is interesting to note that Jim Collins, in *Good to Great*, identified similar characteristics in the greatest American corporate leaders he studied—humility, drive, resolve, willingness to share credit, and willingness to work quietly.[127]

Key themes from my interviews—emphasizing empowerment, viewing individuals as members of larger systems, and recognizing one's own limitations—also have important overlap with a major player from the Majority World, Yunus Social Business (YSB). YSB was founded by Bangladeshi Muhammad Yunus who also pioneered microfinance and founded Grameen Bank. As YSB invests in social businesses, they look for three traits that make the "perfect" social entrepreneur: passion, an ability to attract local talent, and an in-depth understanding of the local community.

Regarding the last trait, "We look for entrepreneurs who are leaders in the community that they intend to reach, who understand the market for the product or service the social business aims to provide." They also insist on including local talent on the leadership team because "no matter how talented the entrepreneur may be, only through the creation of an effective team will the business be able to scale."[128]

To summarize, the collaborative, empowering approach I found to be so valuable in this study often goes against the grain of American culture and against the qualities American organizations look for in social entrepreneurs. Nevertheless, there is strong support for this approach from research cited throughout this book, from YSB, from the outcomes of the five cases described in Chapters 14 through 18, and from the perspectives of the Majority World leaders I interviewed.

WRESTLING WITH POWER

At the core, pursuing collaboration and empowerment are not simply strategies for building a sustainable enterprise. They reflect a central assumption that power must be shared, and that local people hold essential assets if holistic development is to occur. This approach requires an investment of time and a measure of vulnerability. It requires learning and listening. It requires a team rather than an individual approach. In many ways, it requires leaders to operate outside of cultural norms. But this should not be surprising because, frankly, it's not natural to share one's power.

David Brooks, an op-ed columnist with the *New York Times*, wrote about this challenge in *The Road to Character*. He wrote this book in his quest to define his own life's priorities. His observations offer valuable insight into this central issue of motivation.

Brooks writes of virtues you list on your resume and contrasts these with virtues others speak about you at your funeral. He sees similarities between these two sets of virtues and what Rabbi Joseph Soloveitchik described as Adam I and Adam II—opposing sides of our nature. According to Brooks,

> Adam I is the career-oriented, ambitious side of our nature. Adam I is the external, resume Adam.... Adam II is the internal Adam. Adam II wants to embody certain moral qualities, wants to have a serene inner character, a quiet but solid sense of right and wrong—not only to do good but to be good. Adam II wants to love intimately.
>
> While Adam I wants to conquer the world, Adam II wants to obey a calling to serve the world.... Adams I and II

live by different logics. Adam I—the creating, building, and discovering Adam—lives by a straightforward utilitarian logic. It's the logic of economics. Input leads to output. Effort leads to reward. Practice makes perfect. Pursue self-interest. Maximize your utility. Impress the world.

Adam II lives by an inverse logic. It's a moral logic, not an economic one.... Success leads to the greatest failure, which is pride. Failure leads to the greatest success, which is humility and learning.... We live in a culture that nurtures Adam I, the external Adam, and neglects Adam II.[129]

The most effective partnerships require courage and inner strength because the work will regularly push against cultural norms that applaud ambition, outputs, and achievement. During the interviews, a few Americans spoke of this tension as they observed leaders whose work seemed to flow from the Adam I logic of desiring to conquer and impress instead.

One group mentioned were successful businesspeople who had amassed significant wealth and now felt they owed it to society to help others. These individuals had turned to social enterprise to help the world's most vulnerable create wealth of their own. While this type of entrepreneur knows how to create wealth and wants to make it possible for others to do so, they often assume they can *conquer* inequities with their knowledge and expertise, just as they have successfully conquered challenges in the past.

Others mentioned young adults studying global inequities and observing suffering around the world who were prompted to pursue greater justice through development work. While they may have approached their work with a desire to serve, some I interviewed also noted the pride they had observed in these young adults—the assumption that they had answers to the world's problems that older generations had foolishly overlooked. Rather than being driven by humility, the work of these young adults appeared to be characterized by a dismissiveness of all past efforts to address global poverty.

A desire to conquer, a desire to prove oneself or to disprove others—these are Adam I motivators. Effective partnerships instead require a recognition of what you lack and a desire to learn and to submit yourself to others. Sharing power requires leaders who exhibit the Adam II qualities of courage, love, and humility. But these are not qualities that are easily acquired nor qualities that American culture nurtures, according to Brooks.

James Owolabi, a Nigerian, spoke to the significant challenges of living an Adam II life in an Adam I world:

> Why do people live in cocoons in other countries? Fear of looking stupid. You must be willing to be vulnerable, to be misunderstood, to be laughed at because you don't speak the language. Americans aren't comfortable doing that. Most people don't want to engage in the work—in the people, in relationships. They want to be a celebrity.
>
> The best social entrepreneurs don't care about the press they get. Americans are so quick to find a tweet, a video. You don't want to hear the stories. In hearing others' stories, you learn to feel stupid, to mispronounce words.
>
> One of the sad realities is the more you get to know people, the more you learn you are not as different from them as you think. We are all broken. I need you as much as you need me. The average American is just scared to admit that.

To have the courage to do the difficult work of building a sustainable enterprise as part of a multifaceted team, these fears must be named. Many Americans working in international development possess substantial social, intellectual, and financial capital. However, this can simply translate into raw power in most locations. You may not be fully aware of the power you hold, but those more vulnerable around you are usually keenly aware of it. To use that power for good, take the time to identify how external and internal influences shape your work. Taking the time for this introspection can provide you with tremendous insight about your work and may well help you rethink the very work you are doing.

PERSPECTIVES

Do you believe these three impediments to effective partnership play a greater or lesser role when building an enterprise in the United States?

What are your motivations for engaging in development work? Write a statement that expresses your motivation in fifty words or less. Then, ask a trusted friend for honest feedback on your statement.

Twenty-One

A Better Way

"Alone we can do so little; together we can do so much."

Hellen Keller

Before I offer concluding thoughts, a summary of the research findings may be useful. For a variety of reasons that we have explored, broadly speaking, Americans are skilled at innovating, launching businesses, and pushing hard to see quick results. They are also great at achieving goals. Americans value self-sufficiency and tend to be optimistic as they take on big challenges.

People from the Majority World, on the other hand, tend to take a far more patient approach to development and don't feel the same pressure to accomplish things quickly. They generally see themselves as part of an interdependent group rather than primarily as individuals, and many place a much higher value than Americans do on building long-term relationships with clients, customers, and employees.

Approaches to development work reflect these cultural differences. In this study, Americans tended to focus on solving a material problem that plagues a region, while Majority World leaders tended to prioritize empowering people so that they would be able to build a better future for themselves. Leaders from the Majority World do not ignore people's material needs, but their approach often emphasizes holistic restoration. Again and again, they explained to me that if, in the process of solving a material problem, people's dignity is lessened, you may have achieved a short-term gain but you have missed the more crucial long-term need.

Yes, people need clean drinking water, a means to produce more food, and employment opportunities. These are real needs. But even more essential, people repeatedly said, is the need to experience dignity, to feel as if you have something to contribute to the world, to believe your life matters and that you have the agency to make choices for your good and the good of those you love.

Different definitions of the problem to be solved and different cultural norms contribute to different approaches to building an enterprise as the table on the following page shows.

THREE PATHS

How do I hope the reader will change after hearing these voices and seeing many of his or her own assumptions questioned? The takeaway for Americans cannot be work smarter and recognize Majority World concerns about American-led development work so you can become more productive and self-sufficient. That would only continue the individualistic approach to building an enterprise that is culturally natural for Americans, but also deeply problematic.

The message I repeatedly heard from Majority World leaders was not "Change these key strategies to become more successful." Instead, the message was "Recognize our significant cultural

Simplified Contrasts of Social Enterprises

American-Led	National-Led

Goals

American-Led	National-Led
• Success defined in economic terms	• Success defined using human development terms (*e.g.*, empowerment, dignity)
• Focused goals	• Holistic goals
• Focus on scaling, growth, widespread impact	• Focus on community development, local impact

Relationships

American-Led	National-Led
• Power concentrated; strong, guarded leadership	• Power shared; submission to employees not uncommon
• Isolated from nationals they are trying to support	• Proximity to nationals they are trying to support
• Self-sufficient	• Interdependent

Pace

American-Led	National-Led
• Move quickly, action-oriented	• Patient, grow business more gradually
• One- to five-year time horizon	• Time horizon rarely specified
• Proactive American marketing strategies	• Word of mouth dominant

Role of Local Context and Culture

American-Led	National-Led
• Bring in Western innovations	• Improve local technologies
• Focus on individuals	• Focus on both individuals and the community
• Emphasize external culture through introduction of American technologies, business methods, values	• Emphasize liberation of local culture to reach its suppressed potential

differences. Recognize the power dynamics that are at play and their implications for us. Recognize the value of pooling assets."

A takeaway for readers from the Majority World is the picture, in Chapters 14 through 18, of American and Majority World leaders effectively working together, building enterprises with significant impact that utilize team members' distinct assets in both humble and powerful ways. I also hope that this book provides you with a deeper understanding of our cultural differences. Americans operate with speed, focused goals, an emphasis on innovation, and as determined individuals within their own country as well. This approach has both positive and negative implications within America's borders much like it does in other countries. The current unrest and brokenness in American society are leading to soul searching for some and perhaps to foundational changes that will spill over into a broader interest in truly partnering with others. This is reason for hope.

There are three paths from which we can now choose. *Path One* is to "go home," for Americans to leave Majority World people alone with their problems as some are suggesting. It seems unlikely that this path will be followed. The world is too interconnected, but this path is also unlikely because Americans, on the whole, care about suffering people and would have a difficult time just turning their backs on them.

Path Two is to do what is culturally comfortable, to continue to operate from largely parallel tracks that have Americans and nationals working simultaneously but separately. Regardless of who you are, it is natural to operate within your own cultural norms, to primarily tap your own assets, to hold onto power.

For Americans, operating within your cultural norms likely means relying on your own intellectual, financial, and/ or social capital to build an enterprise as you have conceived it. Are there dangers to this approach? Most definitely, including possible harm to those you set out to help. Many Majority World leaders I interviewed believe empowering vulnerable people and communities to deal with the complex problems facing them is the core issue that must be addressed. With this as the goal, Americans' natural approach is not, at its worst, neutral. Moving quickly, independently, and with great optimism, all the while missing contextual cues is not typically a recipe for empowerment. It is more often a recipe for unintended dominance.

For Majority World leaders operating from a collectivist perspective, working closely with outsiders can feel very unnatural and risky. Personal and national history may confirm your concern. Perhaps you are willing to tap a few of an outsider's assets, but building a long-term, mutually dependent partnership with an American seems unwise.

But both Americans and nationals miss the value of the others' assets when we choose not to partner. We miss the opportunity to address together deep systemic issues that challenge all of our societies. We also risk missing, or at least delaying, the opportunity to re-establish relationships under terms that help us all to progress.

AN UNCOMMON PATH

The second path involves operating more safely, from our own cultural norms. *Path Three* involves the challenge of operating from a place of significant discomfort, but from a place that also offers tremendous opportunity.

Bring your assets, every form of capital you have been entrusted with, and become part of a cross-cultural team that shares a passion for working alongside the most vulnerable. This will require developing respect for people who differ in significant ways from you, as well as a good measure of humility as you allow yourself to learn and partner with people your culture says are not always trustworthy or wise. It will also require a slower pace than Americans are used to. However, this approach is worth the risk because of three significant opportunities that partnership holds.

1. The opportunity to build something bigger and better than you alone could build

When you pool your assets with those who have a different asset set, the outcome can be powerful. Chapters 14 through 18 provided examples of enterprises built upon the assumed value of pooled assets.

Klein Ileliji, a Nigerian professor working in the United States, spoke of the value of formally pooling assets to build enterprises together. "We should be training our [American] young men and women to be merging with African young men and women—to form partnerships. Americans bring a global market. They are sensitive to entrepreneurship. They grew up with it."

In this scenario, the pooling involves long-term partnerships. Majority World leaders articulated two additional approaches to combining assets that they believe have merit: providing access to laboratory equipment and production facilities as well as serving in an advisory capacity. Each of these is discussed in turn below.

Access

Laud Basing, whose voice you have heard throughout these pages, is a microbiologist with a desire to lower the incidence of sexually transmitted diseases (STDs) in Ghana and beyond. He launched Incas Diagnostic Services and has developed testing methods that do not require blood.

In addition to his technical skills, Basing understands the culture, the stigma around STDs, and challenges related to the public nature of traditional testing. He also understands people's hesitancy to trust someone with a needle. In his words,

> The person who is going to test you is your neighbor's brother. The pharmacist who you'd go to for treatment is

your sister's friend. There's a stigma with the way we are testing now. Also, testing is invasive because blood work is required.

We need a test kit that is very easy to use—no blood required, and the sample is discreetly acquired. We can't produce these ourselves because of a lack of capacity. I want to produce low-cost diagnostic kits. I don't have the capacity. If I want to produce molecular-based tests, I can't do it.

To develop these different testing methods, Basing has used equipment at various laboratories in the United States, including the Centers for Disease Control and Prevention. Incas Diagnostic Services is making a sustainable, significant difference in Ghana today because Basing was willing and able to team with Americans to develop new approaches to a widespread problem. Like the five cases presented in earlier chapters, this collaboration has proven powerful.

Advising

Advising is another interesting approach to asset sharing. Gambah Kpante and Delia Diabangouaya from Togo have established a chocolate factory there called Chocotogo. They process cocoa beans, chocolate, and cocoa pastes and are hoping to create other products with the beans. One of their roles now, as Diabangouaya described it, is,

Spreading chocolate, candies, and a market for them in Togo. We could grow far more. Ghana and other big countries now grow 70 percent of the world's cocoa beans. Prices are fixed in London by people who don't know the work farmers are doing in the fields. Prices are too low. Farmers just produce and export. One hundred percent of production was raw exports. We are the first company to process cocoa beans in Togo. We work with farmers, telling them the beans they are selling are so valuable.

They don't eat them. An eighty-year-old woman has farmed beans for life but has never tasted the chocolate. What is the impact of the product they are farming? They do not know.

We have two plants of production. The farmers' organization we buy from is already certified organic and fair trade, so we are encouraging them to stay with organic so prices will stay high. Women especially are working at the plants. We are also working with the consumers to help them understand the fun of chocolate, to build a demand for chocolate.

Diabangouaya and Kpante participated in the Mandela Washington Fellowship Program, spending six weeks in the United States to learn more about food production, food science, and business development from American experts. They also wanted to establish connections with professionals who could advise them as they built Chocotogo. They recognized their assets as well as areas where they needed others' expertise if they were going to achieve their goals for their business and their country.

Wilfrid Marx Abidji is part of SENS Benin, an incubator that provides advising, training, and connections to market opportunities for Beninese entrepreneurs. He too is interested in pooling assets with Americans through advising.

From his perspective, "Americans and Europeans have developed many good practices that we want to learn. We won't copy but adapt…. We need mentors."

Cordie Aziz, born in America and now permanently residing in Ghana, affirmed the important advisory role that Americans could play in the Majority World. "Find someone who's already in the movement but doesn't have access to funding, or who needs technical expertise you can share. There are already so many young people doing awesome things in a community."

There is tremendous variety in the form an asset-pooling relationship may take and tremendous potential from the synergy.

2. The opportunity to release creativity and empower vulnerable people

Creating teams that include the vulnerable people you are trying to help can also release the tremendous potential that resides within them. A Sri Lankan NGO leader has learned the path to empowerment from decades of experience. "When you build trust, it leads to more honesty and less lying. The agenda becomes more than tasks. You are forging friendships. When the poor recognize they have something needed to offer, it is very empowering."

Pooling the assets of Majority World leaders, Americans, and the vulnerable people you are trying to serve can also release tremendous creativity. Phil Smith, a leader for the microfinance organization HOPE International, observed this release of creativity firsthand:

> Truly transformational social enterprise is dependent on the hard work, know-how, and training of individuals. The development of that is left up to the individual. Otherwise, when the project ends, things tend to fall apart. I chaired the board of [a savings and credit entity]. As much as we wanted to change their lifestyle quickly, to see them living in nice houses, living with a higher standard, I needed to be very content with allowing them, step by step, to develop their skills and become entrepreneurs. That can be painful....
>
> I would describe the environment as zero capital injection creating dignity and empowerment. Once empowerment is unleashed, once they begin to lose the poverty mindset, there's incredible creativity and incredible things that happen as a result ... The care they

have for each other, subgroups creating an idea and taking out a loan for something.

These are the poorest of the poor. They don't even qualify for a microfinance loan lots of the time. It's an unleashing of a spirit that says, "I can do this. I don't need anyone to help me."

3. The opportunity to help us all flourish

Finally, combining the assets of multiple people as an enterprise is built offers the potential for *everyone* to experience greater flourishing. Think back on the framework for flourishing I presented in Chapter 12, and the evidence I cited that questions whether the American culture is indeed flourishing.

Americans are generally highly efficient, productive, fast-moving people, with a get-'er-done approach. Without a counterbalance, however, have many of us become overworked, stressed, impatient, exhausted, and out of balance in terms of our priorities in life? The evidence I presented about stress levels, rates of depression and anxiety, and isolation would indicate this is the case.

James Olowabi, a Nigerian, shared his concern about Americans after living and working in the United States for twenty years:

I sat down one day and decided the average American doesn't care what I think, what I feel. They just want to get what they can out of me. Once I started thinking like that, I was effective in my workplace. They don't want to build relationships. They just want to make money. They don't care about me as a person.

Americans fundamentally believe that we exist for work. When you get up as a man, the first thing you do is go to work. You work, and you work, and you work, and you don't stop until the work is done. That's what built

America. If you don't understand American strengths, then you don't understand why they struggle so much to help other people's weaknesses.

What if, by partnering with people in the Majority World, Americans were able to observe and experience different, more effective ways of building elements of *our* society and elements of *our* personal lives? Could people from very different cultures offer Americans a needed counterbalance to our current ways of living? There are valuable societal lessons that could be learned from people around the world—racial reconciliation from Rwandans; contentment from Haitians; the value of close community from Colombians (see Junior Auguistin's and Stephen Eyman's commentaries in Chapter 10).

In the same vein, people from the Majority World could benefit from partnering with Americans to learn different ways of living. Regarding time specifically, many from the Majority World are more relaxed, more balanced in the way they divide their time between work and rest. However, without a counterbalance, they can become inefficient and less productive because they don't adhere to schedules and timelines. Mavis Thandizo Kanjadza observed, "I like Americans' idea of time. We need to learn from Americans about the idea that time is money. We waste time. It's a very unproductive and inefficient use of time."

Regarding individualism and collectivism, Americans tend to view people as individuals rather than as members of larger groups. This is a valuable trait to some I interviewed from Majority World cultures who described an inability to work alongside people outside their tribe because of strong ingroups and outgroups.

Wilfrid Marx Abidji from Benin specifically expressed a desire to see people serve others from outside their clan:

Instilling the value, the principle of community service. Because we are used to staying within the clan, we are not building volunteerism in the country. Someone from Oklahoma coming to help make something good happen in Benin … seeing that in action takes you out of the normal way of seeing things.

Junior Auguistin from Haiti also expressed an interest in becoming more like Americans as they encounter outsiders:

I really appreciate the way Americans treat people, the love they have for each other. Sometimes I'm on a hike with some American people, and when they see other Americans in the street, they stop and make conversation. In Haiti, we don't really find that.

What could we learn from each other about reconciliation, about collaboration, about building strong communities if we risked getting proximate?

FINAL THOUGHTS

Americans have valuable resources to help heal some of the brokenness in our world. We have optimism, creativity, and an important sense of urgency to support the world's most vulnerable. In economic terms, we possess important social, intellectual, and financial capital. These are resources that we value, that have brought many Americans economic prosperity. But they are largely valuable resources for solving problems that have material answers, such as safe water.

Majority World leaders in this study were focused on a different kind of problem, one focused on dignity, agency, and empowerment more than electricity or safe water. To address this type of problem, Majority World leaders hold essential capital. They have access to social networks, a deeper understanding of poverty, market knowledge, and a long-term commitment to development. While introducing new material resources into a community can be accomplished alone by outsiders, empowerment can never be.

Americans have ample power and resources to swoop in and address a material problem efficiently and strategically. But too often, our work lessens people's dignity as they are left out of decision-making and as they feel pressured to invest in goods they do not necessarily value. For both cultural reasons and reasons based on power inequalities, the people we are trying to help will likely never tell us no outright.

So, the question becomes, how will Americans choose to utilize the power and resources that we have? We live in a time when power is highly visible, brash, and loud. It is often abused. In this scenario, power is rightly characterized as negative or evil. But power can also be quiet, outside the limelight, humble, and proximate.

I challenge Americans to view the assets you possess as a trust, a vehicle to empower others. As an American, you do not know enough to "fix" others' problems. There are crucial resources for building a truly valuable enterprise that you will always lack. The preceding chapters have outlined the steps involved in taking an uncommon path. First, acknowledge your assumptions about others' needs and your ability to address them. Second, accept your limitations, the skills and assets you do not possess but that are essential for building a lasting enterprise. Third, appreciate others' assets—the skills, experiences, and societal standing that people from the Majority World possess. Finally, align your vision with the vision of those you are trying to serve. A diagram of these four steps follows.

An Uncommon Path Forward

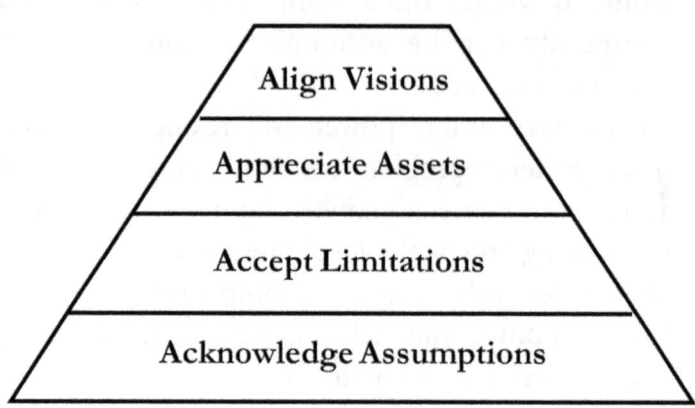

"I have exhausted my savings to make this work." A Rwandan social entrepreneur spoke these words to me, but I heard this statement multiple times from both American and Majority World leaders. People around the globe are passionate about making our world a better place. If this were a simple challenge with straightforward solutions, we would have made far more progress by now both in the Majority World as well as in the United States.

Historical tensions, deep cultural differences, and often a lack of appreciation for others' assets make the development space complex for everyone involved. But these challenges can also drive us to humbly acknowledge our need for others. And that is an excellent place to start.

The findings from this research do not offer simple answers. Instead, they offer a different way of viewing our roles in the world. Each of us is one important player in a much larger story. Our roles are each valuable, and their greatest usefulness is found when lived out in partnership with others.

Appendix

Research Methodology

For interested readers, this appendix provides further details about the research methods that formed the foundation of this book.

GROUNDED THEORY

This study was designed using a grounded theory methodology that relied on inductive reasoning. Interview data were analyzed as the study progressed, using the constant comparative method.[130] Codes were created and revised, patterns were identified, and finally, a conceptual model was developed.

Having conducted research using cultural theories for years, I did not begin this qualitative study with a blank slate. I expected that cultural differences would help to answer one of my key research questions: How and why do American and Majority World leaders differ in their approach and goals for building an enterprise and for international development more generally?

Cultural constructs by Hofstede, Hall, and Meyers (see Chapters 4 through 6), therefore had to be considered from the start. But as Lather described,

Building empirically grounded theory requires a reciprocal relationship between data and theory. Data must be allowed to generate propositions in a dialectical manner that permits the use of *a priori* theoretical frameworks, but which keeps a particular framework from becoming the container into which the data must be poured.[131]

These cultural theories contributed to the questions I asked and helped make sense of what I was learning, but they were not my primary guide for the study. Instead, the interview data itself guided my exploration of how cultural differences played out in development work.

DATA COLLECTION

Because I was using a grounded theory approach, I made decisions regarding the first stages of data collection based on my initial understanding of development work in the Majority World.[132] The sampling method used was snowball or chain referral sampling. I began interviewing people working in Asia, Africa, and Latin America with whom I had an established relationship. I then asked these individuals to refer me to others who also might be willing to share their perspectives around the questions I was asking. This allowed me to access individuals in remote areas as well as individuals from a wide variety of networks.

For almost every interview, I typed the conversation in real-time, capturing approximately 85 percent of the conversation verbatim. After each interview, I immediately read through the transcript, adding skipped words, correcting spelling, and filling in missing details from the conversations, noting that these additions were not verbatim. The conversations averaged an hour in length.

I intentionally chose not to record the interviews because I wanted people to feel as comfortable as possible, especially given the power dynamics that are often part of conversations between Americans and individuals from the Majority World. Research has also found that audio-recorded transcripts and transcripts from notes written during interviews are often similar in detail and the latter may be the preferred approach under some circumstances.[133]

The interviews were semi-structured throughout the study, allowing interviewees to share what they were most passionate about and allowing me to explore in the moment intriguing topics that they mentioned. Most people I interviewed face-to-face in the United States, some I interviewed using Skype, and two I communicated with through voice recordings on WhatsApp. A small number in rural areas of Africa, I am humbled to say, communicated with me by texting on their phone. Also, two students studying international development conducted interviews with eleven American social entrepreneurs which added significantly to the project. In all, we interviewed ninety people from Africa, the Caribbean, Latin America, South and Southeast Asia, and the United States. The table below summarizes the interviewees' regions of origin.

Interviewees' Region of Origin

Region of Origin	Number Interviewed
Africa	35
Latin America & The Caribbean	3
South and Southeast Asia	7
United States	45

DATA ANALYSIS

Using classic grounded theory, data collection and analysis are interconnected rather than distinct phases. After conducting ten interviews, I used QDA Miner software to begin the initial coding of the transcripts. I used codes developed at the start of my research, drawn directly from the questions I was asking, such as "cultural understanding" and "assets."[134] Consistent with the grounded theory method, I used a constant comparative approach to data collection and analysis, reading and rereading transcripts at the same time I was collecting new data, then adding, deleting, and altering interview questions to inform the next iteration of data collection.

In the middle of the data collection process, I was able to talk with several recipients of the Mandela Washington Fellowship for Young African Leaders, social entrepreneurs from across the African continent. According to the website, this program "empowers young people through academic coursework, leadership training, and networking" during a six-week stay at an American university. I conducted interviews as well as four focus groups of three to six people each, which allowed me to learn a tremendous amount as they interacted thoughtfully and sometimes heatedly with each other around my questions.

Following classic grounded theory, I added codes as the interviews and focus groups progressed, reflecting new topics that were emerging such as "heropreneur," "trust," and "hope." This process can be characterized as Open Coding, "The process of breaking down, examining, comparing, conceptualizing, and categorizing data."[135] The questions I asked during interviews also changed and expanded as the research progressed. Beginning with the basic question of differences between American and national-led development work, I expanded my research to explore the following:

- How and why do American and Majority World leaders differ in their approach and goals for building a social enterprise and for international development more generally?
- What are on-the-ground implications of these differences?
- According to Majority World leaders, what are truly beneficial ways for Westerners to engage in the Majority World?

With these expanded and revised research questions, I began to use Axial Coding, putting data back together in new ways by making connections between categories. This process utilizes a coding paradigm that involves "conditions, context, action/interactional strategies, and consequences."[136] I began, for example, comparing enterprises by type of service or product offered, the makeup of its leadership team when it launched and when I interviewed a team member, and by the amount and kind of growth the enterprise had achieved over time.

I then used Selective Coding, which emphasizes validating the relationships among core categories of codes and entails further refinement and development of these categories.[137] For example, "culture" was a core category, but it now encompassed several important sub-categories I had not identified at the start. During the interviews, I heard people describe several ways they interacted with a local culture including working to save or protect it, transplanting or overlaying American culture onto it, and esteeming differences between the American and local culture. This category, I realized, was related to the makeup of an enterprise's leadership team and the extent to which the core problem the leaders were trying to solve was economically based.

At this point, I had interviewed approximately seventy people and I switched to a theoretical sampling approach,[138] pursuing interviews with people working in countries where I had conducted few or no interviews (*e.g.*, Mexico and Haiti). This I did for comparison purposes, wanting to test whether the patterns I was identifying were evident in additional contexts. Focusing on the three central questions listed previously, I found additional support for the hypotheses I was generating.

As another means to test my hypotheses, I contacted twelve people I had previously interviewed to be certain I was capturing their ideas accurately. Once I had a complete draft, three interviewees—one American and two Ghanaians—provided me with invaluable feedback. They too affirmed my hypotheses and challenged me to delve deeper in certain areas, particularly around the topics of justice and the values that most define a culture. This led me to interview the final twelve people for this project. Once I had a final draft, I shared the entire manuscript with an additional six Majority World interviewees to confirm that I had appropriately captured their ideas. The following table provides a summary of the different research phases.

Research Phases

Research Phase	Number of Interviews/ Points of Contact
Phase 1 – Initial Theory Development	55
Phase 2 – Theory Refinement	20
Phase 3 – Member Check	3
Phase 4 – Theory Expansion & Confirmation	12
Phase 5 – Final Member Check	6

Testing hypotheses across multiple world regions, asking interviewees for feedback about my understanding of their statements and my conclusions, and having three people review the entire manuscript were all efforts to assure that the information I had gathered was accurate and matched reality, *i.e.,* was internally valid. External validity, generalizability to other contexts, is not the intent of qualitative research. I do, however, hope that subsequent research by myself and others will test and further refine the key findings of this study.

Notes

Introduction

[1] I have chosen the term "Majority World" to refer to the low-and middle-income countries of Asia, Africa, and Latin America. This term accurately reflects where most of the world's population resides, it conveys a sense of power rather than weakness, and it is easier to read than "lower- and middle-income countries" (LMIC), another term that is used today.

[2] William Easterly, *The White Man's Burden: Why the West's Efforts to Aid the Rest Have Done So Much Ill and So Little Good* (New York: Penguin Press, 2007), 5-6.

[3] Easterly, *The White Man's Burden*, 382-383.

[4] Arturo Escobar, *Encountering Development: The Making and Unmaking of the Third World* (Princeton, N.J.: Princeton University Press, 1995), 4.

[5] For a more complete discussion of the research methods used in this study, see the Appendix.

[6] Alisha Coleman-Jensen, Matthew Rabbitt, Christian Gregory, and Anita Singh, "Household Food Security in the United States in 2021",

No. 309, U.S. Department of Agriculture, 2022, https://www.ers. usda. gov/publications/pub-details/?pubid=104655

[7] "National Center on Family Homelessness," accessed June 5, 2023, https://www.air.org/center/national-center-family-homelessness.

[8] Lane Gillespie, "Bankrate's 2023 annual emergency savings report," February 23, 2023, https://www.bankrate.com/banking/savings/ emergency-savings-report/.

Chapter One: Is Innovation Enough?

[9] "Giving USA 2021," Giving USA, https://givingusa.org/giving-usa-limited-data-tableau-visualization/

[10] "The Index of Global Philanthropy and Remittances, 2016," Hudson Institute, https://www.hudson.org/research/13314-index-of-global-philanthropy-and-remittances-2016

[11] Edward Twitchell Hall and Mildred Reed Hall, *Understanding Cultural Differences: Germans, French, and Americans* (Yarmouth, ME: Intercultural Press, 1990), 153.

[12] "Public Trust in Government:1958-2022," Pew Research Center, https://www.pewresearch.org/politics/2022/06/06/public-trust-in-government-1958-2022/.

[13] Siri Terjesen, "Social Entrepreneurship Amongst Women and Men in the United States," *National Women's Business Council*, (2017) https://cdn.www.nwbc.gov/wp-content/uploads/2017/02/13134000/ Social-entrepreneurship-amongst-women-and-men-in-the-United-States_021617.pdf

Chapter Three: Contrasts

[14] Edward Tylor, *Primitive Culture: Research into the Development of Mythology, Philosophy, Religion, Art, and Custom, Volume 1* (London: John Murray, 1871), 1.

[15] Ken Myers, "Volume 9," *The Mars Hill Audio Journal*, https://marshillaudio.org/people/ken-myers?page=1.

[16] "6D Model of National Culture," Hofstede Insights, accessed June 5, 2023, https://geerthofstede.com/culture-geert-hofstede-gert-jan-hofstede/6d-model-of-national-culture/

Chapter Four: I or We?

[17] Geert Hofstede, "Dimension Data Matrix," accessed June 5, 2023, https://geerthofstede.com/research-and-vsm/dimension-data-matrix/.

[18] Geert Hofstede, *Culture's Consequences* (Thousand Oaks, CA: Sage Publications, 2nd edition, 2001), 226, 227, 236, 237, 244, 245, 251, 254.

[19] Hofstede, *Culture's Consequences*, 213.

[20] Hofstede, *Culture's Consequences*, 250.

Chapter Five: Who's Got Time?

[21] Richard Lewis, "How Different Cultures Understand Time," June 1, 2014, http://www.businessinsider.com/how-different-cultures-understand-time-2014-5#ixzz3XU9CUArT.

[22] Lewis, "How Different Cultures."

[23] Cecil Helman, "Cultural aspects of time and aging. Time is not the same in every culture and every circumstance; our views of aging also differ," *EMBO Reports* 6, Spec No, Suppl 1 (2005): S54-8, doi:10.1038/sj.embor.7400402.

[24] Craig Storti, *Figuring Foreigners Out: A Practical Guide* (Yarmouth, ME: Intercultural Press, 1998), 82.

[25] Erin Meyer, "Comparing Management Cultures," April 25, 2014, https://hbr.org/web/infographic/2014/04/comparing-management-cultures.

[26] David Champion, "A Tool That Maps Out Cultural Differences," April 25, 2014, https://hbr.org/2014/04/a-tool-that-maps-out-cultural-differences.

[27] Edward Hall, *Beyond Culture* (New York: Doubleday, 1976), 91.

[28] Erin Meyer, *The Culture Map: Breaking Through the Invisible Boundaries of Global Business* (New York: PublicAffairs, 2014), 40.

[29] Meyer, *The Culture Map*, 39.

[30] Meyer, *The Culture Map*, 39.

[31] Adapted from Meyer, *The Culture Map*, 39.

Chapter Six: Achievement's Role

[32] "Key Statistics for Breast Cancer," American Cancer Society, June 15, 2022, https://www.cancer.org/content/dam/CRC/PDF/Public/8577.00.pdf.

[33] Max Roser and Hannah Ritchie, "Malaria," October 2019, https://ourworldindata.org/malaria

[34] Arona Maskil, "Understanding American Culture: Tips for Acclimating to US Daily Life," accessed September 12, 2020, https://www.internationalstudentguidetotheusa.com/articles/understanding-american-culture.htm

[35] Hofstede, *Culture's Consequences*.

[36] Hofstede, *Cultures Consequences*, 298, 299, 306, 312, 318.

[37] Hofstede, "Dimension Data Matrix."

[38] Hofstede, *Cultures Consequences*, 279.

Chapter Seven: Starting Points

[39] Norris Krueger Jr. and Peter Dickson, "How Believing in Ourselves Increases Risk Taking: Perceived Self-Efficacy and Opportunity Recognition," *Decision Sciences* 25, no. 3 (May/Jun 1994): 385, https://doi.org/10.1111/j.1540-5915.1994.tb00810.x.

[40] Robert Baron, "Opportunity recognition as pattern recognition: How entrepreneurs 'connect the dots' to identify new business opportunities," *Academy of Management Perspective* 20, no. 1 (February 2006) 104.

[41] Israel Kirzner, *Competition and Entrepreneurship* (Chicago: University of Chicago Press, 1973).

[42] "Asian Proverbs and Old Sayings," The History of Art and The Curious Lives of Famous Painters, accessed September 12, 2020, http://www.historyofpainters.com/asian_ proverbs.htm

[43] "72+ African Wise Proverbs and Inspiring Quotes," Our Afrikan Heritage 2019, http://www.afrikanheritage.com/72-african-wise-proverbs-and-inspiring-quotes/.

[44] "298 Mexican Proverbs," Special Dictionary, accessed June 5, 2023, http://www.special-dictionary.com/proverbs/source/m/mexican_proverb/.

[45] Sorti, *Figuring Foreigners Out*, 51.

[46] "Nathan Myhrvold Quotes," Brainy Quote, accessed June 5, 2023, http://www.brainyquote.com/quotes/quotes/n/ nathanmyhr541325.html.

[47] Kevin Lynch, "Social Enterprise and the Privilege Economy," October 4, 2014, https://www.huffpost.com/entry/social-enterprise-and-the_b_5646091?utm_hp_ref=impact&ir=Impact.

[48] Lexico, Oxford, accessed November 9, 2020, https://www.lexico.com/definition/stratagem.

[49] Lyndon Baines Johnson, (1964). "First State of the Union Address," American Rhetoric Online Speech Bank, https://www.americanrhetoric.com/speeches/lbj1964stateoftheunion.htm.

Chapter Eight: Defining

[50] "Fixes," *New York Times*, accessed September 14, 2020, https://www.nytimes.com/column/fixes.

[51] Travis J. Lybbert and Bruce Wydick, "Poverty, Aspirations, and the Economics of Hope," *Economic Development and Cultural Change* 66, no. 4, (July 2018): 722, https://www.journals.uchicago.edu/doi/abs/10.1086/696968.

[52] Michael Kremer, Gautam Rao, and Frank Schilbach, "Behavioral Development Economics," in *Handbook of Behavioral Economics: Foundations and Applications 2, Volume 2, eds.* B. Douglas Bernheim, Stefano DellaVigna, and David Laibson (New York: North Holland, 2019), 345, https://doi.org/10.1016/bs.hesbe.2018.12.002.

[53] Esther Duflo, Michael Kremer, and Jonathan Robinson, "Nudging Farmers to Use Fertilizer: Theory and Experimental Evidence from Kenya." NBER Working Paper, no. 15131 (July 2009): 35, https://economics.mit.edu/files/6170.

54 Kremer, Rao, and Schilbach, "Behavioral Development Economics," 347.

55 Poverty Probability Index, accessed June 5, 2023, http://www.progressoutofpoverty.org/.

56 Dana Blanton, "Fox News Poll: The American Dream," January 25, 2017, http://www.foxbusiness.com/politics/2017/01/25/fox-news-poll-american-dream.html.

57 "About Haute Baso," Haute Baso, accessed September 14, 2020, http://www.hautebaso.com/

58 "Global Synthesis: Consultations with the Poor," World Bank, September 1999, http://www-wds.worldbank.org/external/default/WDSContentServer/WDSP/IB/2008/12/30/000020953_20081230150555/Rendered/PDF/453500BOX0334096B.pdf.

59 "The African Evaluation Principles," African Evaluation Association, https://afrea.org/AEP/new/The-African-Evaluation-Principles.pdf.

Chapter Nine: Increasing Others' Power

60 Sam Adeyemi, Global Leadership Summit, South Barrington, Illinois, August 11, 2017.

61 Lybbert and Wydick, "Poverty," 722.

62 Jeffrey R. Bloem, Duncan Boughton, Kyan Htoo, Aung Hein, and Ellen Payongayong, "Measuring Hope: A Quantitative Approach with Validation in Rural Myanmar," *Journal of Development Studies* 54, no. 11, (2018): pp. 2078-2094.

63 Lybbert and Wydick, "Poverty," 709.

64 Charles R. Snyder, (2002) "Hope Theory: Rainbows in the Mind," *Psychological Inquiry* 13, no. 4, (2002): 249-275, https://doi.org/10.1207/S15327965PLI1304_01.

65 Anthony D. Ong, Lisa M. Edwards, and C.S. Bergeman, "Hope as a Source of Resilience in Later Adulthood." *Personality and Individual Differences* 41, no. 7, (2006): 1263-73, https://doi.org/10.1016/j.paid.2006.03.028.

[66] Matthew W. Gallagher and Shane J. Lopez. "Positive Expectancies and Mental Health: Identifying the Unique Contributions of Hope and Optimism." *The Journal of Positive Psychology* 4, no. 6, (2009): 548-56.

[67] John Gottman, "John Gottman on Trust and Betrayal," *Greater Good Magazine*, October 29, 2011, http://greatergood.berkeley.edu/article/item/john_gottman_on_trust_and_betrayal/.

[68] David De Cremer, "Understanding Trust, In China and the West," February 11, 2015, https://hbr.org/2015/02/understanding-trust-in-china-and-the-west.

[69] Melinda J. Moye and Alan B. Henkin, "Exploring Associations between Employee Empowerment and Interpersonal Trust in Managers," *Journal of Management Development* 25, no. 2, (2006): 101-117.

[70] Heather K. Spence Laschinger, Joan Finegan, and Judith Shamian, "The Impact of Workplace Empowerment, Organizational Trust on Staff Nurses' Work Satisfaction and Organizational Commitment," in *Advances in Health Care Management Vol. 3*, eds. Grant T. Savage, John D. Blair, and Myron D. Fottler, (Bingley: Emerald Group Publishing Limited, 2002), 59-85. https://doi.org/10.1016/S1474-8231(02)03006-9.

[71] Judith M. Gappa, Ann E. Austin, and Andrea G. Trice, *Rethinking Faculty Work: Higher Education's Strategic Imperative* (San Francisco: Jossey Bass, 2007), 145.

[72] Clayton P. Alderfer, *Existence, Relatedness and Growth: Human Needs in Organizational Settings* (New York: Free Press, 1972).

[73] Cameron Anderson, Michael W. Kraus, Adam D. Galinsky, and Dacher Keltner, "The Local-Ladder Effect: Social Status and Subjective Well-Being," *Psychological Science* 23, no. 7 (2012):764-71. https://doi.org/10.1177/0956797611434537.

[74] Abhijit Banerjee, Esther Duflo, Nathanael Goldberg, Dean Karlan, Robert Osei, William Pariente, Jeremy Shapiro, Bram Thuysbaert, and Christopher Udry, "A Multifaceted Program Causes Lasting Progress for the Very Poor: Evidence from Six Countries" *Science* 348, no. 6236 (2015): 15, DOI: 10.1126/science.1260799.

Chapter Ten: Assumptions

[75] Melinda Gates, Global Leadership Summit, South Barrington, Illinois, August 12, 2016.

[76] "Work and Workplace," Gallup, https://news.gallup.com/poll/1720/work-work-place.aspx.

[77] Jeffrey M. Jones, "In U.S., 40% Get Less Than Recommended Amount of Sleep," Gallup, December 19, 2013, http://www.gallup.com/poll/166553/less-recommended-amount-sleep.aspx.

[78] "Here's Why Some Workers Don't Feel Rejuvenated after Taking Vacation," Qualtrics, March 29, 2022, https://www.qualtrics.com/blog/going-back-to-work-after-vacation/

[79] Bryan Stevenson, Global Leadership Summit, South Barrington, Illinois, August 10, 2017.

Chapter Eleven: Points of Friction

[80] "Top Lifetime Grosses," IMDbPro, accessed September 14, 2020, https://www.boxofficemojo.com/chart/top_lifetime_gross/?area=XWW.

[81] "Alfred Nobel's Will," The Nobel Peace Prize, accessed June 5, 2023, https://www.nobelprize.org/alfred-nobel/alfred-nobels-will/.

[82] Max Fisher, "The Amazing History of the Nobel Prize, Told in Maps and Charts," *Washington Post*, October 15, 2013, http://www.washingtonpost.com/blogs/worldviews/wp/2013/10/15/the-amazing-history-of-the-nobel-prize-told-in-maps-and-charts/.

[83] "Bill Gates' Shocking Personal Attacks on Dr. Dambisa Moyo and Dead Aid," May 28, 2013, YouTube, https://www.youtube.com/watch?v=5utDdxveaJc.

[84] Bruce Wydick, Paul Glewwe, and Laine Rutledge, "Does International Child Sponsorship Work? A Six-Country Study of Impacts on Adult Life Outcomes," *Journal of Political Economy* 121, no. 2. (2013): 400.

Chapter Twelve: Power That Prevails

[85] "The Future of World Religions: Population Growth Projections,

2010-2050," Pew Research Center, April 2, 2015, http://www. pewforum.org/2015/04/02/sub-saharan-africa/.

[86] "Religion in Latin America: Widespread Change in a Historically Catholic Region," Pew Research Center, November 13, 2014, http://www.pewforum.org/2014/11/13/religion-in-latin-america/.

[87] "The Changing Global Religious Landscape," Pew Research Center, April 5, 2017, http://www.pewforum.org/2017/04/05/the-changing-global-religious-landscape/.

[88] Jubilee Centre, accessed June 6, 2023, https://static1.squarespace. com/static/62012941199c974967f9c4ad/t/621ced4772a7da2fd429eb cd/1646062921275/Jubilee+Roadmap+-+Jubilee+Centre+-+2019.pdf

[89] Hofstede, *Culture's Consequences*, 12.

[90] Andy Crouch, *Culture Making: Recovering Our Creative Calling* (Westmont, IL: InterVarsity Press, 2013), 26-27.

[91] Amy Novotney, "What's Behind American Consumerism?" American Psychological Association, July/August 2008.

[92] Jonathan Walton, "Jesus, Chief Executive: The Gospel of Health and Wealth at the Core of American Religion," Lake Institute Lecture, March 31, 2016, https://philanthropy.iupui.edu/institutes/lake-institute/programs/.

[93] Hofstede, *Culture's Consequences*, 254.

[94] "Social Isolation and New Technology: How the Internet and Mobile Phones Impact Americans' Social Networks." Pew Research Center, November 4, 2009, http://www.pewinternet.org/2009/11/04/social-isolation-and-new-technology/.

[95] Daniel A. Cox, "The State of American Friendship: Change, Challenges, and Loss," American Survey Center, June 8, 2021, https://www.americansurveycenter.org/research/the-state-of-american-friendship-change-challenges-and-loss/.

[96] "The Loneliness Epidemic Persists: A Post-Pandemic Look at the State of Loneliness among U.S. Adults," Cigna, accessed June 5, 2023, https://newsroom.thecignagroup.com/loneliness-epidemic-persists-post-pandemic-look.

97 Lydia Anderson, Chanell Washington, Rose M. Kreider and Thomas Gryn, "Share of One-Person Households More Than Tripled from 1940 to 2020," U.S. Census Bureau, June 8, 2023, https://www.census.gov/library/stories/2023/06/more-than-a-quarter-all-households-have-one-person.html

98 Niraj Chokshi, "Americans Are Among the Most Stressed People in the World, Poll Finds," *New York Times*, April 25, 2019, https://www.nytimes.com/2019/04/25/us/americans-stressful.html.

99 "Anxiety Disorders - Facts and Statistics," Anxiety and Depression Association of America, accessed June 6, 2023, https://adaa.org/understanding-anxiety/facts-statistics."

100 "Life Expectancy in the U.S. Dropped for the Second Year in a Row in 2021." August 31, 2022, https://www.cdc.gov/nchs/pressroom/nchs_press_releases/2022/20220831.htm#:~:text=Life%20expectancy%20at%20birth%20for,2020%20to%2073.2%20in%202021.

101 Steven H. Woolf and Heidi Schoomaker, "Life Expectancy and Mortality Rates in the United States, 1959-2017," *Journal of the American Medical Association* 322, no. 20, (2019): 1996–2016. doi:10.1001/jama.2019.16932.

102 James R. Doty, "The Science of Compassion," *Huffington Post*, August 7, 2012, http://www.huffingtonpost.com/james-r-doty-md/science-of-compassion_b_1578284.html.

103 Carolyn Zezima, "Incarcerated with Mental Illness: How to Reduce the Number of People with Mental Health Issues in Prison," Psycom, August 12, 2020, https://www.psycom.net/how-to-reduce-mental-illness-in-prisons.

104 "Criminal Justice Fact Sheet," National Association for the Advancement of Colored People, accessed June 6, 2023, http://www.naacp.org/criminal-justice-fact-sheet/.

105 "Charts that Explain Wealth Inequality in the United States," Aspen Institute, October 19, 2022, https://www.aspeninstitute.org/blog-posts/charts-that-explain-wealth-inequality-in-the-united-states/.

106 "Trust in Federal Government Branches Continues to Falter," Gallup, accessed June 6, 2023, https://news.gallup.com/poll/402737/trust-federal-government-branches-continues-falter.aspx.

[107] "Public Trust in Government: 1958-2019," Pew Research Center, April 11, 2019, https://www.pewresearch.org/politics/2019/04/11/public-trust-in-government-1958-2019/.

[108] Jeffrey M. Jones and Camille Lloyd, "Larger Majority Says Racism Against Black People Widespread," Gallup, July 23, 2021, https://news.gallup.com/poll/352544/larger-majority-says-racism-against-black-people-widespread.aspx.

[109] Commission on Legal Empowerment of the Poor and United Nations Development Programme, "Report of the Commission on Legal Empowerment of the Poor, Volume 1" (2008): 1-2, https://www.un.org/ruleoflaw/files/Making_the_Law_Work_for_Everyone.pdf.

[110] Gary Haugen, "The Poor Deserve Equal Protection by the Law," January 26, 2014, https://www.washingtonpost.com /opinions/the-poor-deserve-equal-protection-by-the-law/2014/01/26/e2f40a8a-8556-11e3-bbe5-6a2a3141e3a9 _story.html?utm_term=.8bc7ef59f0fa.

[111] Crouch, *Culture Making*, 29-30.

Chapter Thirteen: Distinct Assets

[112] Crouch, *Culture Making*, 56-57.

Chapter Sixteen: IMON International

[113] "Who We Are," Mercy Corps, accessed June 6, 2023, https://www.mercycorps.org/who-we-are.

[114] Katherine W. Phillips, "How Diversity Makes Us Smarter," Scientific American, October 1, 2014, https://www.scientificamerican.com/article/how-diversity-makes-us-smarter/.

[115] Sangeeta Badal, "The Business Benefits of Gender Diversity," Gallup, January 20, 2014, http://news.gallup.com/businessjournal/166220/business-benefits-gender-diversity.aspx.

[116] David Rock and Heidi Grant, "Why Diverse Teams Are Smarter," *Harvard Business Review*, November 4, 2016, https://hbr.org/2016/11/why-diverse-teams-are-smarter.

[117] Stephen Turban, Dan Wu, and Letian Zhang, "Research: When Gender Diversity Makes Firms More Productive," *Harvard Business*

Review, February 11, 2019, https://hbr.org/2019/02/research-when-gender-diversity-makes-firms-more-productive.

[118] Harvey M. Wagner, Report: The Bottom Line: Corporate Performance and Women's Representation on Boards (2004-2008), Catalyst, March 1, 2011, http://www.catalyst.org/knowledge/bottom-line-corporate-performance-and-womens-representation-boards-20042008.

[119] Sangeeta Badal, "The Business Benefits of Gender Diversity," Gallup, January 20, 2014, http://news.gallup.com/businessjournal/166220/business-benefits-gender-diversity.aspx.

Chapter Twenty: Impediments to Partnership

[120] John L. O'Sullivan, "The Great Nation of Futurity," *The United States Democratic Review*, 1839, https://www.mtholyoke.edu/acad/intrel/osulliva.htm.

[121] Stan Nussbaum, *Why Are Americans Like That?* 2nd edition (Morton, IL: Enculturation Books, 2013), 84-85.

[122] "Venture: Selecting Our Ashoka Fellows." Ashoka, Accessed June 6, 2023, https://www.ashoka.org/en-us/program/venture-selecting-our-ashoka-fellows.

[123] "Skoll Awards," Skoll, accessed September 16, 2020, http://skoll.org/about/skoll-awards/.

[124] Sarah Zak Borgman, "The Power of Proximity: Envisioning a Shared future," Skoll, December 19, 2017, http://skoll.org/2017/12/19/the-power-of-proximity-envisioning-a-shared-future/.

[125] David Bornstein, *How to Change the World: Social Entrepreneurs and the Power of New Ideas* (New York: Oxford University Press, 2007), 233.

[126] David C. McClelland, "Characteristics of Successful Entrepreneurs," *Journal of Creative Behavior* 21 (1987): 219-233.

[127] Jim Collins, *Good to Great: Why Some Companies Make the Leap … and Others Don't* (New York: HarperCollins Publishers, 2001), 20-36.

[128] "3 Key Characteristics of Great Social Business Entrepreneurs," *Forbes*, December 18, 2013, https://www. forbes.com/sites/ skollworldforum/2013/12/18/3-key-characteristics-of-great-social-business-entrepreneurs/#18bcfb14f60c.

[129] David Brooks, *The Road to Character* (New York: Random House, 2015), xi – xiii.

Appendix: Research Methodology

[130] Barney G. Glaser and Anselm L. Strauss, *The Discovery of Grounded Theory* (Chicago: Aldine Publishing Company, 1967).

[131] Patti Lather, "Research as Praxis," *Harvard Educational Review*, 56, no. 3, (August 1986), 267.

[132] Glaser and Strauss, *The Discovery of Grounded Theory*.

[133] Rwamahe Rutakumwa, Joseph Okello Mugisha, Sarah Bernays, Elizabeth Kabunga, Grace Tumwekwase, Martin Mbonye, and Janet Seeley. Conducting in-depth interviews with and without voice recorders: a comparative analysis. *Qualitative Research* 20, no. 5, (October 2020): 565-581. doi: 10.1177/ 1468794119884806.

[134] Matthew B. Miles and A. Michael Huberman, *Qualitative Data Analysis: An Expanded Sourcebook, 2nd Ed.* (Thousand Oaks, CA: Sage Publications, 1994).

[135] Anselm Strauss and Juliet Corbin, *Basics of Qualitative Research: Grounded Theory Procedures and Techniques.* (Newbury Park, CA: Sage Publications, 1990), 61.

[136] Strauss and Corbin, *Basics of Qualitative Research*, 96.

[137] Strauss and Corbin, *Basics of Qualitative Research*.

[138] Glaser and Strauss, *The Discovery of Grounded Theory*.

Glossary

Culture – A complex whole which includes a society's knowledge, beliefs, laws, morals, customs, wisdom, and vision of a life well lived.

Majority World – The low- and middle-income countries of Africa, Asia, and Latin America, reflecting where most of the world's population resides.

Non-Governmental Organization (NGO) – Organizations which are independent of government involvement and are often focused on humanitarianism; typically a nonprofit entity.

Social Enterprise – A business whose primary aim is social good rather than profit maximation.

Chapter Summaries

Introduction
Tensions between nationals and Americans can be significant as Americans engage in development work in the Majority World. This study set out to identify the roots of these tensions as well as constructive steps forward that better address critical differences in our goals and approaches. The study's findings have important implications for work with marginalized groups in the United States as well.

Section 1 – Differences
Cultural differences can be dramatic, making it much easier to segregate than to work side by side. Nevertheless, both people from the Majority World and the United States bring valuable perspectives to the work of building a positively impactful enterprise.

Chapter 1 – Is Innovation Enough?
Americans want to help vulnerable people in the Majority World and tend to be quite generous, but we often build

enterprises using strictly business or technical expertise. We must understand facets of the work that go beyond strategy and tactics. We must understand cultural differences, differences in priorities, and the importance of partnering for all involved.

Chapter 2 – Healthy Living
The risk of not understanding vulnerable people's priorities and values is failure, as the case presented in this chapter illustrates.

Chapter 3 – Contrasts
American and Majority World social entrepreneurs often pursue quite different outcomes through their work. As a result, their approaches differ in important ways. Two cases highlight several of these differences.

Chapter 4 – I or We?
American culture is highly individualist, while most Majority World cultures are collectivist. This difference greatly influences the nature of the relationship between the enterprise and its employees and customers, as well as leaders' primary goals for their work.

Chapter 5 – Who's Got Time?
Americans tend to view time as linear and finite while people from many Majority World cultures view time as fluid and infinite. The appropriate pace for building an enterprise and the expected time horizon for achieving goals can therefore vary substantially.

Chapter 6 – Achievement's Role
People from masculine cultures, particularly the men, value quantifiable goals, broad impact, and efficient use of resources. Individuals from feminine cultures, and many women from

masculine cultures, emphasize relationships and training that promotes each employee's dignity and agency. These values are often at odds with each other as scarce resources are allocated within an enterprise.

Chapter 7 – Starting Points
An assumed internal or external locus of control, one's historical context and proximity to the problem, and how the challenge is framed by the social entrepreneur all shape expectations and the level of optimism that is brought to the work.

Section 2 – The Problem to Be Solved
There is an important relationship between our cultural values and the problem we seek to solve through an enterprise. Differing problem definitions often lead to friction and power struggles between Americans and those they are trying to help. Unnamed assumptions that drive a leader's work add complexity to the situation.

Chapter 8 – Defining
Americans and people from Majority World countries often define the problem they are trying to solve quite differently as evidenced by what they measure, their vocabulary, and their values. Americans tend to focus on addressing material problems while those from the Majority World tend to emphasize empowering individuals and communities.

Chapter 9 – Increasing Others' Power
In the interviews, people from the Majority World mentioned power differentials far more often than Americans did. They also frequently prioritized empowering the people they were trying to help by building hope, respect, and trust. Overall, Americans were less apt to emphasize empowerment through their work.

Chapter 10 – Assumptions
According to Majority World leaders, Americans and those from the Majority World often operate under different assumptions as they build an enterprise. Social distance, optimism, a fast pace, and a belief that people around the world share similar aspirations keep many Americans unaware of foundational differences.

Chapter 11 – Points of Friction
In this study, different cultural backgrounds, goals, and assumptions led to friction in seven key areas related to building an enterprise: 1) the pace of work; 2) the nature of business relationships; 3) the role of innovation vs. restoration; 4) the definition of appropriate marketing strategies; 5) the value assigned to scaling; 6) the priority of individual vs. community values; and 7) the role of law and nature of ethics.

Chapter 12 – Power That Prevails
Problems facing any society are complex and involve many interconnected pieces. American-led enterprises operating in a Majority World country may survive despite deep friction, but unintended negative outcomes can result from their presence. Americans must acknowledge their own weaknesses and look honestly at the change they hope to bring about in another society, because there is a cost associated with every change.

Section 3 – Partnership
Combining the assets of American and Majority World individuals often leads to enterprises that neither party could have built alone. There are barriers to this collaborative approach, but also great opportunities for everyone involved.

Chapter 13 – Distinct Assets
People working in development must come to terms with others' strengths and their own limitations. American and Majority World individuals each possess distinct and valuable assets.

Chapter 14 – 18 – The Synergies of Partnership
These chapters present five cases of social entrepreneurs who successfully shared power and built enterprises that local people have embraced.

Chapter 19 – Three Key Assumptions
Leaders of these five social enterprises shared three common assumptions: 1) our enterprise must emphasize empowerment; 2) employees and customers are members of important community systems that must not be ignored; and 3) we must recognize our personal limitations if we are to build a sustainable enterprise. Leaders incorporated eleven practical approaches in their work based on these three assumptions.

Chapter 20 – Impediments to Partnership
People interviewed for this study highlighted three factors that often work against effective partnerships: 1) American media's portrayal of Majority World countries; 2) American foreign and domestic policy that too often favors the powerful; and 3) the common desire among social entrepreneurs to be a hero.

Chapter 21 – A Better Way
Based on these findings, the reader has three paths from which to choose: 1) go home, 2) build alone, or 3) build with others. Building with others offers perspectives and assets that could allow everyone to experience greater flourishing.

Index

Note: Boldface entries refer to tables and figures.

GLOBAL RESILIENCE PUBLISHING
and PIPPA RANN BOOKS & MEDIA
imprints of
SALT DESERT MEDIA GROUP LTD., U.K.
*Working in collaboration with international distributors
from the whole of the English-speaking world.*

Salt Desert Media Group Ltd (est. 2019) is a member of the Independent Publishers Guild. At present, the company has two imprints, **Pippa Rann Books & Media (PRBM)** and **Global Resilience Publishing (GRP)**.

GRP began operations in Autumn 2021, with the first publications planned for release in 2022. As the name suggests, the imprint focuses on subjects such as:

- Climate Change
- The Global Financial System
- Multilateral Governance (e.g., the United Nations)
- Public-Private Partnership
- Leadership around the World
- International System Change
- International Corporate Governance
- Family Firms around the World

- Global Values
- Global Philanthropy
- Commercial Sponsorship
- New Technologies including Artificial Intelligence

Two things make GRP unique as an imprint:

1. Our books take a global perspective (not the perspective of a particular nation);
2. GRP focuses exclusively on such global challenges.

By contrast, **Pippa Rann Books & Media (PRBM)**, launched on August the 17th, 2020, publishes books by people of Indian origin on any subject, but focuses on India, and on the Indian diaspora. Please see the list of books already published, and the books forthcoming from PRBM, at www.pipparannbooks.com

Both GRP and PRBM are open to first class ideas for books, provided complete manuscripts can be turned in on time.

Please note that GRP and PRBM exclusively publish material that nurtures the values of democracy, justice, liberty, equality, and fraternity.

***

Global Resilience Publishing and **Pippa Rann Books & Media** are only two of several imprints that are conceived of, and will be launched, God willing, by Salt Desert Media Group Ltd., U. K. The imprints will cover different regions of the globe, different themes, and so on. And if you have an idea for a new imprint that you would like to establish, please get in touch.

Prabhu Guptara, the Publisher of Salt Desert Media Group, says, "For all our imprints, and for the attainment of our incredibly high vision, we need your support. Whatever your gifts and abilities, you are welcome to support us with the most precious gift of your time. The service you do is not for us but for the sake of the world as a whole. Please email me with your email, location, and phone contact details, letting me know what you feel you can do. Could you be an organiser or greeter at our events? Could you ring people on our behalf? Write to people? Write guest blogs or articles? Write a regular column? Do interviews? Help with electronic media, social media, or general marketing? Connect me with people you know who might be willing to help in some way or other?"

He adds, "I am one man, so I do not and cannot keep up with everything that is happening. There are many challenges and numerous opportunities – help me to understand what these are. Pass information on to me that could be useful to me. Put your ideas to me. Any and all insights from you are most welcome, as they will multiply our joint effectiveness. It is only as we work together that we can contribute effectively to changing our world for the better".

***

Join our mailing list to discover books from Global Resilience Publishing which will inform you on a wide range of topics, inspire you, and equip you as an individual, as a member of your family, and as someone who wants to make the world a better place.

www.globalresiliencepublishing.com

Printed in the USA
CPSIA information can be obtained
at www.ICGtesting.com
LVHW011518061223
765857LV00001B/1/J